By Invitation Only

by

Gail Higgins

DREAMCATCHER PUBLISHING
Saint John • New Brunswick • Canada

Canadian Cataloguing in Publication Data

Higgins, Gail - 1941

By Invitation Only

ISBN - 1-894372-11-5
        I. Title.
    PS8565.I426B9 2003   C811'.6   C2003-901965-9
    PR9199.4.H54B9 2003

Editor: Yvonne Wilson

Typesetter: Chas Goguen

Cover Painting   Artist: Lyn Van Tassel
                      Location: Shamper's Bluff, New Brunswick

Cover Design: Dawn Drew, INK Graphic Design Services Corp.

Printed and bound in Canada

DREAMCATCHER PUBLISHING INC.
1 Market Square
Suite 306 Dockside
Saint John, New Brunswick, Canada E2L 4Z6
www.dreamcatcher.nb.ca

For my wonderful children and their generation
whose goodness and openness
fill me with hope for the future.

With special thanks to my husband, Len - my mentor and my best friend.

I have a deeply moving memory from the early days of our local peace group. The plan was to have our first walk through the uptown area. We would be led by a police car and finish with a rally in the Square. My role on that day was to lead the marchers - an idea which terrified me more with each passing moment.

At the agreed upon hour my husband leaned over and said, "Let's go. It's time." This very private, remarkable man walked shoulder to shoulder with me - not because he wanted to be there, not because he belonged to our peace group and not even because he agreed with my tactics. He was there because I needed him to be there. I will never forget that act of love and support.

Again we walk shoulder to shoulder...

Acknowledgments

To Terry Comeau, whose wisdom, editorial guidance, support and friendship meant more to me than words can say.

To Pam Bourque, whose gracious generosity and patience transformed stacks of longhand into a working document on disc.

To Sue Hooper, whose creative guidance and encouragement inspired me.

To Brigitte Ledermann, whose wise counsel, warm support and professional expertise made the preparation of the manuscript a pleasure.

To Peter Ledermann, whose technical problem-solving was very helpful.

To Elizabeth Margaris, Yvonne Wilson and *Joan Allison*, whose openness to new ideas and first time authors makes DreamCatcher Publishing an exceptional company. I'm deeply grateful for the warmth of their welcome, their confidence in me and their vision for "By Invitation Only." Special thanks to Yvonne Wilson, author, editor and friend, who guided this book to completion.

To *Lyn Van Tassel*, whose lovely painting graces the cover and to the owners of this original work for sharing it with me.

"*I want facts. I demand them as my right. I want to know if there be a personal God. If so there be, I want to know His will about me. I want to know about the instructions I find written upon my soul, and I am anxious to find if He has given any further instructions in the course of time.*

I want to know where I came from, where I am going, and how I should get there. I want something solid and immovable to stand on. I want a platform. Facts will give it to me." (1)

James Leonard McGuire, 1927.

I Believe (1994)

I believe
>That life is not a test
>That love transforms
>That people are equal
>That our limitations are self-imposed
>That everything is sacred
>That power is meaningless
>That questions have answers
>That my mind is free
>That my spirit is free
>That God is real

Section One

Prose

"I know You're there
Just beyond my grasp
Reaching out
Always inviting me to take another step..."

The Beginning

Sometimes it's hard for me to imagine that anyone will believe and accept what is written in this book. I wonder how I would react if these experiences were not my own.

I cannot explain this book. It is what it is. I don't understand the how or why - yet I accept it. That is what makes the book possible for me. I didn't write it, I experienced it. It is my record of those experiences that I offer for your consideration.

I think the ideas in this chapter will seem less extreme when you see how they evolved over the years in the experiences and the poems.

If I have it right, if it is truth, I expect it will be recognized as such because we all have the capacity to recognize truth. If that does not occur - well - so be it. Everything will unfold in whatever way it was intended.

I think I have always believed in the existence of God although my experience of that relationship has covered a wide spectrum. Over the years I have gone back and forth between a close, loving and wonderful connection, to a distant place where I seemed to be pacing alone, almost circling the idea of God. It seemed to me that I was wrong or missing something in my understanding of Him.

God didn't seem to make sense to me, yet Jesus did. In an almost haunting yet beautiful way I found Jesus to be consistent, loving, challenging, courageous, simple. I listened intently to the stories about Him and then I waited to see His reaction in each story. What did He say? How did He handle that situation? He did make sense. There was a clear and deep logic to His words and to His behavior and I felt deeply drawn to that. I kept returning there for answers when everything else "religious" confused me.

The logic of God was much harder, if not impossible, for me to follow. There were so many questions and contradictions that seemed very far removed from sacred mystery - and from personal experience. I wondered how a loving Creator could judge and condemn His creations. I could not reconcile that with my experience of a mother's love.

Why was "God" so unlike Jesus? What kind of God would set up life as a test that we either pass or fail, and why does He need my praise? Does my God really see me as a sinner and want me to plead for mercy?

It seemed to me that many of the characteristics I had come to attribute to God sounded remarkably like our human failings.

When I was in my forties I began to have many questions about human existence as well. Everything else in creation appeared to have an order and purpose. I could not believe that God intended us to live and die in a state of confusion about the meaning of life. We had been given intellect and free will. What was the purpose of these great gifts? If it's true that we use only ten percent of our potential, what is the other ninety percent for? Could it be that we have a level of potential that we have not begun to comprehend?

I wonder if one of the obstacles blocking this realization is a sometimes distorted sense of self. It seems to me that, at times, we may have misunderstood God's message to us. I think He is telling us how strong and wonderful we are - not how weak and sinful.

Sometimes I think about my faith as a kaleidoscope. The basic elements remain the same but they are frequently reshaped so that they fall into place in a new way. Sometimes the changes are profound so it's like entering into the stillness and the mystery from some unfamiliar place. Slowly I begin to find my way - again.

I have never studied philosophy or theology. Sadly the great thinkers of the past are barely more than names to me so I know little of their ideas or discoveries. The thought has crossed my mind that this may have been a significant factor in allowing me to be open to everything.

At some point I seem to have entered into an agreement with God. I can almost remember that agreement happening because I remember understanding my part, but only my part, in it. I know my part involved giving these experiences the top

priority in my life without passing my personal judgement on
their value. I think my part was a commitment to trust God
absolutely, to be open to His movements in my life and to write
down what I understood to be happening.

A way seemed to open up for me which I followed because
it was offered to me. I trusted it and it flowed easily although in
ways new and strange to me at first. This was simply my way,
not better than anyone else's but maybe different. I opened up
to new experiences because I began to have them. I sensed that
I was safe and loved and being invited by God to take another
step. It has been a graced and incredible journey thus far but
not one I seemed to choose - rather, pure gift.

These graced moments would happen with an ease and
peace and joy and certainty and gentleness that had no element
of ego or fear. If I experienced fear it happened in a conscious
moment when I forgot that I was safe and protected, as we all
are. Because these moments were so wonderful - actually,
incredible beyond words - a part of me always longed to return
to them so I sought opportunities to do that.

I have no idea how anyone else's mind works, but maybe I
should say a few things about my own. My mind seems to
wander all over without discipline or focus. Maybe for this
reason meditation and contemplation are not a big part of my
life. That did not seem to matter.

During the 1980's, I was deeply concerned about the threat
of nuclear war. That fear was coupled with the pain of a growing
awareness of human suffering around the globe - preventable
human suffering. How could we justify the global cost of the
arms race in the face of these unmet human needs? I felt these

issues passionately yet these feelings were never expressed in my writing, at least not directly. That surprised me.

I went through a period of serious disillusionment, or maybe it was a serious search for truth as I abandoned the "givens" of my life one at a time. Everything that I questioned seemed to fail the test. It wasn't that everything was bad or wrong; on the contrary - everything was right to varying degrees but never totally, and the flaws were glaring. I wanted to find one thing that was real and unchanging, one thing that I could trust absolutely.

I think this all started as I learned more about all governments, about war, about the military-industrial complex and the weapons trade, about power and greed. All the lines began to blur. I didn't know who spoke the truth. I became suspicious of words. I don't think I was demanding perfection. Errors in judgement, weakness and mistakes were always very understandable to me, knowing them first-hand as I did. It was more about integrity - about unwavering integrity.

During the same period five dear relatives and friends were facing death - slowly and prematurely. That was acutely real, not a time for empty platitudes. I wanted to know something about where they were going. Was there a God, a Heaven, a Hell?

As I write, I realize my search sounds more intelligent and purposeful than it was. In truth, it was a sad, empty, gray time. It didn't matter to me whether I had the skills or the right to ask these questions. It was my life, my mind and I would continue to question and doubt everything until I found something that was true.

I should add that I was near the top of my own list of things being questioned. What was my truth? What would I go to the wall for? I had discovered within myself one thing which sometimes astonished me - a kind of love and a depth of love that I didn't know existed there. I realized that I would go to the wall for my children but I didn't know how to build my life around that reality.

And then there was Jesus. I was respectful but open to discovering that He didn't take close scrutiny either. But that did not happen. The more I listened and read and questioned, the more certain I became of the truth of Jesus. I soon realized that I had to stay very close to Him in my thinking if I were to find answers and personal peace. If I strayed too far from Jesus, the young Jewish man, the carpenter's son, I had the sensation of losing my connection to truth again.

As time passed I became more attuned to and respectful of my thoughts and more aware of what was happening around me. It became very clear to me that the gentle guidance I sought was being given but I was not setting the agenda. It made no difference whether I was in noise or silence at the time of an experience. In some miraculous way these experiences would happen and then I would calmly go on with the routine of my life. Somehow, I could let them be. My thinking was always altered in the sense that I knew whatever I had learned was true, was truth, but I couldn't maintain that level of awareness and understanding. I often forgot temporarily what I had learned but it remained in place somewhere within my consciousness like a building block. It would resurface in memory at the right time or be there for reference. It seemed to become something I could use in daily living from that moment on. My trust in what I was learning was absolute. When I didn't understand something, that was fine too. I knew I would understand at some point.

I have discovered that the only time I am able to write is when I'm writing about these spiritual thoughts and experiences. They push me to start writing. In the beginning I made several futile attempts to write about other subjects and quickly learned that I had no other inspiration.

Another thing I realized was that if the thoughts didn't flow, if I was rephrasing or restarting sentences, I didn't "have it" so I would let it be. Often the thought I was trying to focus on at those times was not the final thought. It was simply leading me somewhere.

Occasionally I would know, somehow comprehend the words of one sentence and I would start writing. The words would flow so clearly and easily that I felt these poems or reflections were not of me but through me. Since I didn't know where any poem was going I was often deeply touched, sometimes to tears, when I read what I had written. The poems became a source of guidance and inspiration for me. I still turn to them often to remember what I know.

I don't feel I'm supposed to start editing thoughts from years ago although it is very tempting to do so. If I were writing everything from my present perspective, I would make a few changes along the way but I think this book is meant to show a progression or a deepening of understanding over the years, so I will leave the words alone.

As I said, although I cannot explain this book I accept it.

That is what makes it possible for me. I didn't "write" it as much as I "experienced" it and tried to record those moments. It is my record of those experiences, thoughts and questions that I offer for your consideration. I believe my experiences are, in many ways, universal. I believe it is only our level of awareness that differs and that that difference is only temporary. Each experience in this book, which includes the poems, should be understood as separate. They were written usually weeks and often months apart and were complete unto themselves.

"Here
Now
Pay attention
I am here
Now"

Chapter Two

In 1984 I began to realize that something was not working in my life. I felt deeply drawn to respond to causes of great human need. In fact, I felt I had a clear responsibility in that area. As well, I recognized that I had very important and ongoing responsibilities as a wife and mother - to say nothing of meeting my personal needs. I began to have a vague sense of being so busy that nothing was really being accomplished. I couldn't see or hear or understand at that speed. Also, I had a sense that everything was repeating itself. Somehow, it seemed hollow - like empty, repetitive words and actions.

Having lost my ability to achieve a healthy balance in my life, almost reluctantly I followed the advice of a friend and sought spiritual guidance. Although I was warmly received by my counselor, weekly meetings felt, at the time, like one more thing to cope with - another commitment of time that I didn't have. My conversational prayers would sometimes reflect this restlessness verging on annoyance, with comments like "God, when did it stop being enough just to be a good person?" and "I don't know what You want from me."

One afternoon in the spring of 1985 I was taking a quiet break alone in my home. I wasn't thinking about anything in particular, when passing through my thoughts came three statements made with a first-person authority:

"I AM ASKING MUCH OF YOU

I HAVE GIVEN YOU MUCH

I WILL ALWAYS BE WITH YOU"

As the last sentence ended, my mind seemed to become alert and focused. I knew something had just happened but I wasn't sure what that "something" was. I remembered the three sentences clearly and repeated them many times. The strangeness of what had happened made me feel a little frightened and isolated, because I felt it was far out of the realm of the ordinary and maybe the normal. Sometimes I worried a bit about the **"ASKING MUCH"** of me part but not too often, or too deeply. Yet I began to feel very comforted by the words and I could be at peace with the fact that they had happened. I felt that my questions to God had been answered in a way that quieted my mind and filled me with a deep peace. Those words have become a precious touchstone for me, an always present source of comfort and strength.

In retrospect, it seems much more than coincidence that my relationship with God changed dramatically only after I took the first step. I turned toward Him for guidance in sorting out my life. It seemed that all I needed to do was show a little willingness toward Him. Even to ask questions acknowledged that He might really exist and be listening.

*"...these spaces are strange
beyond me in every way..."*

Chapter Three

In the spring of 1986 I was relaxing with a friend who was telling me a story. I remember that it was about an elderly man and I think it was about levels of consciousness. I remember thinking that I believed in levels of consciousness but knew little about it.

As we were sitting at my dining room table, I had an incredible experience of openness or expansiveness. I felt it. I knew it. It just *was*. I didn't have any sense of movement from here to there. I was here and then I was there. The closest physical comparison I can think of is the sensation of falling backward off a tree limb or a railing, what you feel the split second you sense that you have lost control of what is happening. The only difference was that, instead of that flashed sense of "down", it was a sense of "up" - happening in a blink.

My friend continued talking. I could see her talking. She

appeared to be lower and a bit farther away than she had been. I knew and could see in perfect detail so much more than she was saying. In my mental image, people were moving; one man was walking with a dog. It seemed I knew and could effortlessly absorb at once every detail. I remember thinking, "I even know what kind of shoes he's wearing."

I was also very aware of myself. I knew I was having this incredible experience and I loved it. I felt happy, absolutely wonderful. My mind was filled with and fully alive in these various images. I didn't see or need to see my body because I knew who I was. I felt complete and whole. I clearly remember thinking, "This must be what it's like when you die." I also remember thinking, "Now I see how God easily knows everything at once." There was no sense of time or space. Everything seemed to co-exist.

Finally I became conscious of both time and space again. I knew that the experience was going to end. I knew things would be as they were before, and I felt sad. I had a sense that my mind would again be so limited and one dimensional that it would seem like being locked in a prison - a human prison. I sensed I had to move down and to the right. The feeling of sadness was the last of this experience. I have no idea how long the experience lasted. My friend appeared to register nothing unusual and yet I remembered every single detail. I could hardly believe it had happened.

I thought, "God has given me a moment of expanded consciousness", and I thought about it, for the most part, as a thrilling experience. Then the memory of one year earlier came immediately to mind and made everything easier to accept:

"I AM ASKING MUCH OF YOU

I HAVE GIVEN YOU MUCH

I WILL ALWAYS BE WITH YOU"

Thinking about this experience later, I really didn't know what to do with such an extraordinary happening and I had a moment or two of panic that maybe I was losing touch with reality, but those moments were very short-lived. What remained was a calm and happy memory of an experience which I loved but didn't understand.

"I entered into the stillness
And knew the tenderness
Of Your presence…"

Chapter Four

The Sunday following my experience of "expanded consciousness" I went to Mass and genuflected, as usual, before entering the pew. I was about six rows from the front on the Tabernacle side of the Church. As I genuflected I glanced at the Tabernacle. I'm not sure I know what happened next but the truth of that moment is the central core of my life - my starting point of truth.

The Tabernacle door and the area in front of it were glowing with a light I really cannot describe with words. Somehow the incredible softness of light seemed to enfold or encompass me. I became part of it. I don't know words that would describe how loved, how exquisitely precious I felt.

Without a thought or a sound I understood that my name had been spoken - my own personal first name - "Gail". I would have turned to answer that call from anywhere in the world. I seemed to be in total stillness, in awe, but I remember feeling a desire to fall to my knees - literally. I felt that I was in the presence of my God.

Again, I was in that moment, then I was in the pew - no in-between. My first thought after this experience seemed almost beyond my comprehension. God knew me! He knew my name! I was overwhelmed but thrilled by that realization - as much as I could absorb it at the time.

I glanced again at the Tabernacle and recognized something that almost took my breath away. It brought the experience of the previous week forward to that moment. It was the exact, identical, matching symbol - as much as matching finger prints or puzzle pieces would go together. It was something that I *knew*.

I think that was the first time I had ever noticed the design on the Tabernacle door, a circle in the upper half of the door containing the symbol for Christ. (The CHI-RHO symbol for Christ, ☧, is an ancient monogram derived from the first two letters of the Greek word for Christos.) Rays emanated from the circle. I knew that somehow I had been in that circle. I also knew that God was in the circle - somewhere.

My first and strongest desire was a deep longing for silence. I wanted to kneel in front of the Tabernacle - just to "be" in the presence of God and the memory of the experience. The activity of the Mass and the presence of the congregation seemed to be in my way. Then I remember feeling torn between a desire to be still and prayerful and a desire to follow my confused and racing thoughts as I tried to sort everything out. I noticed that the sun was shining brightly and I wondered, for an instant, if what I had seen was a glare of reflected light on the door but I knew that was not true. I looked around to see the reactions on other people's faces but they seemed relaxed and normal.

Everything I had thought I knew up to this point in my life, everything I thought I believed seemed to have shifted in that morning of experiences. Truly, the changes were profound and I am still working my way through them.

My prayers from that time on were different. I felt humbled to be in the presence of my God. I was filled with awe and respect. It was a new experience of prayer for me - being still and open before the mystery of God. Many times I have tried to return to that space of stillness and openness. When I succeed, I recognize that my success is not my doing but another gift to me from God.

Some of my beliefs, or at the least some of my thoughts prior to this experience, were in conflict with what I learned that day. I did not find what I thought I was searching for. To be very honest, this is the last thing I would have wanted to find, in one way, because I thought it would be the most divisive. I have always felt quite comfortable with and respectful of any religion or individual life that was based on the principles of Love. I don't think I was really searching for truth in my faith or anyone else's as much as I was hoping for unity. Clearly one of the major problems that separate Christians is the Catholic belief that bread and wine become the Body and Blood of Christ in the Consecration. I have often prayed for an increase in understanding at that Eucharistic point in the Mass because it seemed I could seldom make that last step of understanding. Sometimes I had a sense and an acceptance of the Sacramental mystery. Other times it seemed more like a beautiful, symbolic act of remembering the death of Christ and why it happened.

Now years of thinking in that way dissolved in an instant. These were experiences that I had lived through so I had a deep personal sense of their truth for me.

I knew that the God of my experience of "expanded consciousness" was the same loving God of this Tabernacle experience. He had made that connection very clear to me. So I knew what I knew. I had my starting point.

I knew that God was somewhere in the unconscious where that freedom and joy and knowledge and very real sense of self were. Understanding that, all my Holy Card images of God disappeared. I could let Him be faceless and be comfortable with that.

At this point, I knew that there was something real and living and present about God's connection to us through the bread and wine - although I didn't understand that connection.

Then I thought about Jesus saying, "This is my body" at the Last Supper. If God was to be found in the consecrated bread and Jesus declared Himself to be there also, then I knew that Jesus and God were truly connected - in consecrated bread. Later I wondered what "consecrated" really meant. Did it mean to make sacred? One sacred body? One sacred body of creation?

Over the weeks and months that followed I tried many times to relive that Tabernacle experience in my mind but I could not. Every other image I have had and shall relate in this book I can describe, usually, with ease and clarity; but repeatedly my attempts at recall would produce the same image. What I would see was like a magnified square, like an insert placed in the corner of a larger picture, but it was the only part I could focus on. It was made up of countless perfect circles of light, each one separate and complete but part of the whole. I had the sense that the incredible light, the oneness of light of my experience was actually made up of these perfect circles of light.

That image always seemed to annoy me because I wondered whether that was something from my mind and not from God at all. Also, I think I was somewhat frustrated by my inability to recapture the Tabernacle experience in my memory. All that I was able to remember was what I knew and what I felt. I have never counted on the image of small circles of light to be true. I don't know if it is.

"...We share this moment
Relaxing together
Breathing the same air
I rest in You..."

Chapter Five

During the summer of 1986 I made a seven day silent retreat, the first of my adult life. The natural beauty and serenity of the area were deeply satisfying. I had a sense of being alone with God as I walked the wooded trails, along the shore or sat in silence on the empty beach with the sunset and the birds. One evening, after yet another magnificent sunset, I remember breaking into spontaneous applause. It surprised me but I laughed because I wondered if God was bowing or maybe He was saying a very warm and loving, "You're welcome!"

The fourth night of the retreat I had a dream which destroyed all sense of calm and peace and was as disturbing after I awoke as it had been during sleep.

I hesitate to make public something as private as a dream but this one was different in many ways, particularly in the events that followed it.

I have interpreted the dream many different ways over the years without being sure of any of these interpretations. Sometimes I wonder if it was a "message dream" which I read about somewhere. In any case, I include it here.

A dream I remember vividly

I was standing on a sidewalk with grass-covered hills leading down to the Detroit River on my right. Across the river was the magnificent skyline of the city of Detroit.

I understood several things. Peter seemed to be someone I knew. He had married again and he had a baby. I had a sense that everyone was very happy for him and I was too but I heard the baby wasn't doing well. What I had heard was that he had "failure-to-thrive" problems.

Walking toward me on the sidewalk was Peter's second wife with a baby. I didn't know her but, somehow, I thought her name was Betty. She was holding the baby up against her right shoulder so I was looking at him from the back. They made a lovely mother and baby picture.

When she reached me I walked around behind her shoulder to talk to the baby. I was absolutely horrified. I couldn't believe my eyes. The baby was dying. He was pale and weak and almost lifeless.

I said a number of things. Nobody heard me. There was no reaction to what I said, not even from the mother. I felt that I cried out, "Do something! Babies don't die from 'failure-to-thrive'. That's crazy! Love him more! Maybe he's cold. Wrap him warmer. It just doesn't happen that babies die from 'failure-to-thrive', especially not if you recognize it and define it. You can do something!"

At some point I turned and looked down at the rolling embankment beside me. I saw a high chain-link fence at the bottom and a square concrete building behind it. The water was on the other side. I seemed to sense that businessmen from the building were very annoyed. It seemed that their annoyance was directed at me but I wasn't sure why. I felt that they wanted me to stop what I was doing, to behave myself. They seemed to think what I was doing was nonsense.

Looking to the left I saw a large gathering of people who were having a noisy, happy picnic with clowns and balloons. Little toddlers were crawling around and playing on the grass. Everyone was happy to be there, including Peter's wife - BUT THE BABY WAS DYING! I couldn't believe that people didn't seem to know or understand or care.

The baby was dying but he was not a beautiful or even normal baby. I wanted him to be but there was something very wrong with his face. His eyes were closed but he didn't look like a real baby. His face was slightly distorted as if maybe it was starting to melt. Still, I seemed to feel that he had a weak and almost lifeless body. He desperately needed someone to care for him.

I saw the mother and baby, who was still in the same position, walking where a murder had happened, on the same block and on the same side of the street. They were heading in the direction of my house but I didn't know where they were going. I saw them walking there and I said, to myself, "That's a dangerous block. Someone was murdered there." I didn't sense immediate danger but I felt worried because of the murder. The mother didn't seem to know or care.

I was sitting in my childhood home on the edge of our living room sofa facing the front hall. I seemed to be anticipating something. I felt strangely nervous and kind of sick inside.

I had a sense that I was not alone. Whoever was with me in the room gave me a hint of fear. I seemed to feel it was my mother.

The front door burst open and in came a very cheery, talkative person. I recognized her as Peter's wife Betty but she looked different. She had not spoken to me or to anyone that I recall, and she didn't have the baby. I still thought she was Betty but I don't know why I did.

Even though it was my home she walked briskly through the hall, into the kitchen and back out again. She was talking non-stop but I don't remember anything she said.

By this time I was arriving at the living room doorway. Only then did I notice that my friend Kathy had entered. She was dressed in soft, loose clothing of pale and simple grays and browns. She had obviously come into the house with Betty but had remained quietly at the door. She seemed to find what she saw rather unpleasant. I felt a bit embarrassed and defensive. I had the feeling that she was sad and maybe confused about why I would be part of such a shallow conversation.

I said, "Oh, Kathy, I didn't know you were here." I didn't invite her in and she didn't come in but she didn't leave.

Betty began walking toward me. I backed up to the sofa as she chattered away. She didn't acknowledge Kathy or my mother but seemed intent on talking to me. I was aware that she was very well dressed and not unattractive but she talked too much. I thought she was as warm and nice as she was able to be. I felt no animosity toward her but I did feel somehow detached from her. She confused me.

She was facing me as I sat beside her on the sofa. I asked her how Peter was doing. I was very concerned about him and how he would cope with the tragedy of a dying baby. She said when Peter realized the truth about his baby he was devastated; he cried. She said, "He's doing better now. He realizes and accepts the fact that the baby will die."

At some point in the transition to becoming fully awake and alert I remembered the words "Peter's baby must die."

I found those words very frightening. I tried to tell myself that the sentence must have been "Peter's baby is dying" - but I knew that wasn't so.

When I awoke in my room at the Retreat House everything in and around me seemed to be in a state of disarray. I couldn't seem to clear my mind of this dream. My bedding was dragging on the floor and I was running late so I hardly had time to wash my face. I don't remember going to Mass so I don't know whether I was late for Mass or breakfast in the dining room. On the previous mornings I had been up early and started the day in a quiet, organized way.

I ate my breakfast in silence, as usual, but I couldn't seem to clear or focus my mind. It seemed full of the emotion and the details of the dream but not in a way that would allow me to analyze it. It was like a fog of fullness.

Perhaps this encounter with a person who was on the same retreat will demonstrate what I mean. After breakfast she stopped me in the hall and said she had an interesting experience to relate. I remember feeling surprised that she was talking to me on a silent retreat. After Communion, she said, she had her head down and was deep in prayer when her thoughts were suddenly interrupted and she looked up. As she did so she saw me returning from Communion. She "wondered whether it was God or the evil one" who had caused the distraction until she noticed I had on a T-shirt with "PEACE" written on the front in many languages. She realized then that that was what God had wanted her to notice.

Although I was looking right at her and heard every word she said, I didn't have the slightest glimmer of an idea of what I might say in response, so I said nothing. After an awkward moment or two she smiled and left.

I walked into the Chapel and sat down. I asked God whether I had had a dream or a nightmare and whether I should pay attention to it or ignore it. Then I remembered a comment made to me several weeks earlier which surprised me at that time because I had never heard it before. A woman I know said she always asks God for confirmation when she is making decisions and she receives it. So I said, "God, if this was a message from You, then please confirm it for me."

I sat for a while, maybe fifteen minutes or so, but my mind remained in the same state. Feeling a little tired and frustrated I stood up to leave. As I started moving across the pew, something very soft and flowing rolled across my thoughts. Just two words but I understood them – **"NOT YET."**

I sat down again. After another ten or fifteen minutes when nothing had happened I left the Chapel and walked to my room. To my surprise there was a white envelope with my name on it stuck in my door.

I opened it and pulled out a postcard.

Boston Skyline at Sunset

      The picture on the postcard was a scene from my dream! I was holding the confirmation that I had just asked for. It seemed that there was some incredible freeflow of levels of consciousness going on but I couldn't begin to grasp what was happening. I seemed to be in some "space" I couldn't understand or control. I remember feeling profoundly shocked but I don't recall how that manifested itself physically.

I turned the postcard over and saw that it was blank and old. It was beginning to discolor around the edges. My sense of confusion deepened.

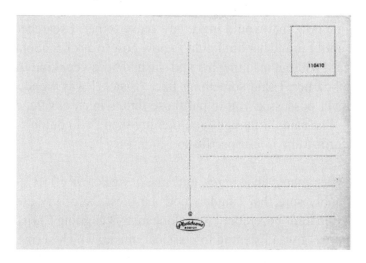

Also enclosed in the envelope were a prayer printed on a card, a small wooden Crucifix and a lovely note. I carried the Cross with me in my pocket until one day, many months later, it wasn't there.

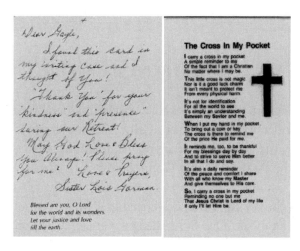

I forget the term that was used as we began the retreat but Sister Gorman had been paired with me or assigned to me although we had no communication until this note. I was sure that God had inspired her to enclose the postcard but I couldn't imagine how that would make any sense to her. I searched all over until I found her but I didn't know how to ask her about the postcard without insulting her and she had been very kind. After I thanked her, I said something like, "Sister, I was wondering whatever possessed you to put those things in an envelope for me?" She said, "I thought you'd enjoy them." I couldn't find the words to be more specific so I didn't try.

After many false starts and many weeks of effort I was reasonably sure that I understood the message of my dream, finally. In mid-December I was alone in my car going Christmas shopping. I was listening to classical music, which seemed to put me in very deep thought. I remember that I had been thinking about a number of Christmas questions such as, What did Christ *really* bring into this world? What are the gifts of Christmas anyway? What does the 'Peace of Christ' really mean?

My thoughts were suddenly and strongly interrupted by one sentence:

"FAILURE-TO-THRIVE BABIES DIE."

That sentence terrified me. I realized in that moment that I had not understood my dream at all… Christ was not the baby. I was. My life might be in danger. Maybe I had to die. Maybe that was the **"MUCH"** that God would ask of me.

Over the winter a friend advised that I listen to some tapes on dream analysis. One thing the speaker suggested on the tape was to try to revisit, in real life, the scene of one's dream. Since my childhood home was twelve hundred miles away, the chance of doing that seemed remote.

During the summer of 1987, however, I flew home because of a family illness. Before leaving Windsor again I drove down to the neighbourhood of my childhood, of my dream. I walked down to the park at the foot of my street. I had a strange sense, one of awe and reverence, that circumstances had unfolded in a way that allowed me to walk in the very footsteps of my dream!

The hills leading down to the water in this area are fairly steep and narrow - a rather small flat area and then a rolling drop to the next level. Much as I always loved the waterfront and the view, I was never too fond of this particular area. It didn't feel safe or welcoming to me. It would be a very inappropriate place for a picnic because it was too small and too dangerous. The little ones could fall and roll down to the next level.

As I walked around the area I spoke to only one person, a fellow stroller. As we both leaned against the railing looking out at the river, we talked about life in the 1950's. I spoke about growing up in that river area and I told him, in general terms, about my dream and retracing my steps. He talked about the realities of being black in Windsor at that time. His story was painful to hear.

Two recent memories while preparing this book have reminded me of why that area felt threatening to me in my dream. In both cases I behaved in ways very much out of character for me. I was trying to be something I was not, trying to imitate other people.

There was a steep gravel hill that ran down to the water beside the grass-covered hills. Often I had seen others ride their bikes down that hill to watch men fishing. At that time there was no railing and the river was deep with dangerous currents. Actually, I remember how the water lapped over the top of the concrete edge. That image always bothered me.

One day, when I was alone in the area, I decided to cruise down that hill even though I knew, at some level, that it might be beyond my skills. As my bike picked up speed I lost control on the gravel and skidded to a halt sideways on my right leg just as I was about to land in the river. To say I was terrified is a gross understatement but I didn't say a word about it to anyone. I wonder if this experience was connected to the physical risk to the children on that hill in my dream.

The second memory is of an event which happened during a brief and unlikely friendship I had with a classmate in Grade School. We were very different but I did like her and I was surprised and happy that she seemed to like being with me.

One day we ended up down by that waterfront building. It was dark and we were talking to a group of boys, most of whom were strangers to me. Everybody was smoking and swearing and the talk was all about drinking and sex. That doesn't seem very shocking to me now but, at the time, I felt very threatened by it - especially since my friend had more to say than anyone. I remember how desperately I wished I were in my own home, in the safe and familiar surroundings of my own bedroom. Perhaps this experience connects to the chastising attitude of the businessmen in my dream.

My street ran perpendicular to the river and my home was several blocks up the street. When I was young someone had been murdered in a house within those blocks.

I continued to walk around the neighbourhood. I stood and stared at the place where my house had been before it was torn down. My home had a living room and a large hall across the front of the house. The sofa was against a big front window and next to a large, old-fashioned floor radio. Behind the radio was the wall which blocked the front door from view and led to the opening into the living room from the hall. If you walked straight from the front door you would walk through the hall and into the kitchen.

I could only say to God that I was trying to observe everything, that I was deeply grateful for the experience but that I still didn't understand my dream.

The following week I had a morning of experiences which were extraordinary for me. I was back home and driving in my car when the word "house" kept recurring in my thoughts. I had a very strong urge to write something down. All I knew was that it would be about a house.

When I returned home I wrote the words which flowed from that thought. I don't know now whether I carried the "house" metaphor too far in my enthusiasm or whether all of the words were gifts of insight to me. On a few occasions I have become so taken with writing the words of a poem that I have lost my quiet focus on the thought. In each case, I am left with a certain detachment or indifference toward the words. That is how parts of this poem have struck me over the years. But I am comfortable with letting the words be. In any case, this is what I wrote:

The house is yours
My gift to you
I have entered because it is also My house
I made it for you
But I will honour your decisions
If you wish to leave
There are other rooms
Other exits
I will remain
And long for your return
Living here is not an accident
I know what will make you happy
If the rooms don't please you
We can decorate them together
They will feel comfortable
Peaceful
Once you have made the home
Truly
Uniquely yours
It will be your greatest joy

Will you invite Me in

Do you wish to live somewhere else
I put you on this street
I took you off this street
This house is no more

But you are
You are not in your house
Your house is in you

I was thrilled by the thought that God was making Himself real and present in my life. He seemed to be giving me words to write which came from a thought which came from a dream. I felt very close to God in that moment of recognizing a mixing of levels of consciousness, again. Actually, I felt euphoric.

Then I remembered all the other things I had written and stuffed away in books and drawers all over the house. For the first time I wondered seriously if God was trying to tell me something in those writings. I decided to try to find each piece of paper and put them in chronological order so I could better understand a message if there was one. As soon as I had that thought, the word "book" began repeating in my mind as "house" had. I picked up a blank piece of paper and wrote across the centre "BY INVITATION ONLY". At the bottom I wrote, "a book".

My first thought about the title seemed to happen as I read the words on the page. I was amazed at the choice of that title because it seemed to define perfectly our relationship with God and His with us. I remember thinking, "That's really clever!" as a detached observer. That paradoxical sense of intimate involvement yet detachment was one I would come to know well. The idea of a book seemed to have a "Well, isn't that strange!" effect on me but I don't remember much else.

I was so thrilled by the morning's events that I decided to celebrate by taking two of my children to a beautiful ocean beach in an area where the high tides are dramatic.

Sometimes things I sense or think, like some of my thoughts as I walked along the water's edge, are so subtle that they feel like no more than a hesitation or a double take in my thoughts. It's like the feeling we have in a conversation when we sense a slight change in someone's facial expression or in the inflection of someone's voice. It's very subtle but we know it happened.

As I walked, my thoughts were still full of God and a happy confusion about all that had gone on. I glanced up at a cliff which marks the far side of the cove where we were. Since it was low tide the moist rocks were exposed down to the low tide line. Slowly I became aware that I was walking underneath the ocean, on the ocean floor - and I felt awestruck - and deeply privileged. I knew that in a short time my view of the cliffs and my footsteps would disappear under water that was three stories high. In that instant I sensed some movement in the rock face in front of me. In a very easy, natural way I broke into a smile of recognition at this moment of connection. I felt I had just exchanged some kind of "Hello again" greeting with God. I have no idea what happened but I remember the impact on me very clearly. Later, sitting on the sand, I wrote the following words:

> I saw You today
> Again
> As I walked along the shore
> The tide was almost out
> And I recognized You
> I was looking at thirty feet of teeming life
> Only a speck of what exists
> Under the surface
> You allowed me to see You
> "you who have eyes to see"
> Before becoming invisible again
> Exposing only dry rock

And lush vegetation

Most of the world is water
Most of me is water

Are You water

The most essential element for life

Are we sand

Billions of us
Since time began
You were here first and always
Shaping and reshaping
Forever beyond human control

When I returned home, I began to collect the reflections I had written over two years. When I saw them again I remembered when I had written each one so I put them in order and identified them by year. Eventually I felt I had found them all. Several days later I began a very serious search for something else. In the process I found another poem. Almost with a smile I thought, "You're amazing, God. Thank you." At that point I lost all interest in continuing my search for whatever else it was. That type of experience has happened to me a number of times since then.

Over the years I began to become more aware of a spiritual longing in others - a search for something more. That left me with mixed feelings - certainly confusion, usually a hint of fear and yet a deepening sense of purpose about putting my understanding of God "out there" in the arena of spiritual thought and discussion. That seemed a reasonable thing to do. Since the insights were gifts to me, I felt an increasing responsibility to share what I understood to be true.

I had a vague understanding that my writings belonged in a "book" that would happen at some time. And it would be called "By Invitation Only". Slowly the idea of this book became more compelling, maybe even essential, to me.

I told myself the worst that could happen was that the book would be ignored. In lighter moments I told my family that we could have a huge bonfire with the unsold copies and roast marshmallows. But, in truth, it has been a long road to move from my private thoughts and writings to being open and public about them. In this on-going process I am sometimes hit by waves of panic, but they pass. Somehow, in the midst of my own fear, I feel safe. The unfolding of my relationship with God is my top priority; the writing of this book has had to take its place among the ongoing challenges and demands of my life.

2002

I'm not sure when I began to have a vague memory of the book I had been reading the evening before the dream occurred in 1986. It was *Be Not Afraid* by Jean Vanier (2). I recalled reading something about Simon Peter but, for some reason, I didn't check it out any more deeply than that.

Only now, as I reread Chapter 4 "Grow" of *Be Not Afraid*, am I struck by the possible connection between Vanier's words and my dream.

He says "In many ways the story of Peter is our story; he represents many of us." In the last paragraph of this chapter Jean Vanier says, "There is a tendency for each of us to look at others, wanting to imitate them… instead of following Jesus."

"...Be empty
Be still
Be led
Listen"

Chapter Six

Sometimes experiences which move me deeply or challenge me to think in a new way come in the form of questions. These moments simply "appear" in my life. The information and inspiration may come through articles, books, movies or people, as well as in moments of quiet reflection, but the effect is the same. A new question arises for me. A new possibility opens up. Perhaps this has happened all through my life (all through everyone's life?) but I had not been aware of it before.

Within a short period of time I moved from one to another of these many questions. In some way each was connected to the other. Each was connected to Scripture. Each altered my thinking. I don't have answers but I would like to share the questions my experiences evoked.

In the fall of 1987 I read a book called *Blessèd Assurance - At Home with the Bomb in Amarillo, Texas* by A.G. Mojtabai (3). Although I came to the book through the peace network, it ended up having serious religious implications for me. Before this, I hadn't given much thought to the place and the effect of Scripture in our lives.

The author wanted to explore the thinking of a community

that had come to peace with the presence of Pantex in their lives. This was the final assembly plant for all the nuclear weapons in the United States. As I recall, during her investigations for her book she discovered the contradiction of a peaceful, family-oriented community with the nuclear weapons plant operating in its midst behind a barbed wire fence. What surprised me was that this community of approximately 160,000 people had over 200 actively supported churches in its midst.

While the author, who is a Jew, interviewed members of this community, she did not declare her religious background, unless asked.

She said "… the habit of turning, at convenience, from New Testament to Old suggests an indiscrimination that conflicts with belief in the progressive development and refinement in the unfolding of God's revelation to man, a "progression" from Old to New, to which all Christians pay at least lip service. Most strikingly, this indiscriminate way of reading conflicts with the disposition of Jesus, whose method was one of selection and critical evaluation. Discrimination was the hallmark of that method - to extricate the spirit from the letter, the intention of a deed from its outward aspect, the essentials of the law and the prophets from the reams of rulings."

She writes "… the constant recourse to the Old Testament (to the most bellicose sections)… strangely negates the "good news" of the Gospels …" It seemed that many of these Christians were "writing Christianity off as something that did not, could not work…".

To the frequent comment that nothing will be solved until Jesus comes, she gave her "constant refrain" - "But Jesus came."

I was stunned by the realizations that this author awakened in me. I do believe in the progressive development of revelation. How could Christians of deep faith believe so many things that appear diametrically opposed - all in the name of God - all through the teachings of Jesus? How could we be so confused when God was not? What is the truth of Christianity?

Since I know very little about Scripture in general and the Old Testament in particular, I decided to attend a Bible Study class, which started in February 1988 (4). For the Exodus event, we used 1250 B.C. as an approximate date with the understanding that future discoveries may allow greater accuracy of that date. But the point that this was a real historical event when God intervened, thus uniting history with faith, was a strong point in the course.

At the very time that we were studying the Exodus the following article appeared in the Globe and Mail, "Biblical exodus a myth, archeologist suggests" (5).

Evidence from Sinai

Biblical exodus a myth, archeologist suggests

BY STEPHEN STRAUSS
The Globe and Mail

Evidence from recent excavations in the Sinai desert indicates there was no exodus by Jews from Egypt, an Israeli archeologist says.

Eliezer Oren, a Ben-Gurion University professor who, from 1972 to 1982, oversaw the excavation of 80 sites in the Sinai peninsula land bridge that links present-day Egypt and Israel, said his research indicates that Egypt controlled the area during the time when the exodus is generally supposed to have occurred — 1300 to 1275 BC.

The excavations, Prof. Oren said, show the Egyptians had established a heavily fortified corridor in the coastal area known as The Ways of Horus to link itself militarily and commercially with provinces that stretched as far north as present-day Syria.

According to the Old Testament, the Jews, through divine intervention, left their slavery in Egypt by passing through a parting of water. They wandered through a desert and arrived in a promised land roughly identified today with Israel. They were then supposed to conquer this land.

Prof. Oren, who was in Toronto yesterday to give a speech on his findings, said his conclusions

EXODUS — Page A2

Exodus called myth

● From Page One

contradict the biblical account of the escape from Egypt.

First, he said, the supposed crossing of the Red Sea would not have taken the Jews out of an area of Egyptian control. "The Egyptian presence in the area is so overwhelming that, if you crossed the Red Sea, you still would have been for all intents and purposes in Egypt."

More important, he said, there are many Egyptian accounts of the region that include no mention of people moving through the area, which archeologists have found to be the only inhabited site in the Sinai at the time.

The Ways of Horus, Prof. Oren said, was such a well-charted and protected domain that Egyptian records are able to track the movements of two runaway slaves.

"They were spotted and the biblical account of 2.5 million people with 600,000 of military age weren't? This can't be explained unless you invoke miracles here, and I am a member of the department of archeology and not of miracles."

He said other recent excava-

tions indicate that cities that were supposed to have been conquered by the Israelites according to the Bible were not even in existence at the time.

The same applies to the only readily identifiable place they arrived at during their wanderings, the town of Kadesh, he said. "To our great surprise, there is nothing there earlier than the tenth century."

He added: "As far as ancient history and archeology goes, the exodus has not been substantiated."

Prof. Oren's conclusions are supported by other archeologists.

"It is a perfectly logical reconstruction and one to which I would subscribe," University of Toronto archeologist John Holladay said.

Prof. Holladay has excavated Tell el-Maskuta, the remains of the Egyptian city of Pithom. Pithom is identified in the book of Exodus as one of the treasure cities that the Jews built before leaving Egypt.

His excavations, however, indicate there was nothing there before the sixth century BC.

I brought the newspaper article to class to ask about it. That became another in my long list of questions. The priest who was teaching the class was a kind and gentle man but, at the time, I felt I was testing his patience as well as that of the class. Sometimes I would look around the table and see how good and bright and devout these people were as they listened in silence to all that was said. I wondered what was wrong with me that I always had to be searching for answers. I didn't even know the questions. As if I could ever find the answers anyway! Who did I think I was to question such teachings? Although the priest made several references to my many questions, he was generous enough to say that I kept the class "interesting."

In March something came up about male circumcisions and Father mentioned that female circumcisions are performed even today in some cultures. I had heard that before, but most people in the class had not. He commented on how barbaric they are with disastrous results for the women.

I had an overwhelming sense of being unable to listen - unable to tolerate the comments. The subject was so horrible - the pain so impossibly intense - that I couldn't stand it. It wasn't my pain but it was a total awareness of the pain that I seemed to have.

At that moment, I had a mental image of two men holding a black woman while the circumcision was performed by a third man. They were on the grass in front of tall trees and I was standing back a short distance. I seemed to be looking through my own eyes, aware of people on my left and right, aware of being in a group. There was no sound but I knew that this woman was conscious and in unspeakable agony.

At the same time I was very aware that I was still in the meeting room surrounded by the others discussing the horrors of female circumcision. I wasn't in any personal physical pain but I felt close to hysteria. I knew I had to do something - maybe run screaming from the room. I thought, "If one more person says anything more about circumcision, I'm going to yell, 'Stop! I can't stand it!'"

The comments ended. I was instantly, deeply calmed. I could hardly believe the intensity of the experience and I wondered what had happened and why. In my notes from that time I wrote "In retrospect, I recall only one circumstance when I have ever felt like that - so close to being out of control. That was during my last few pains of labour before giving birth."

It would be humanly impossible to experience that depth of emotion followed instantly by total calm. For this reason, I believe this was an experience from God. I wondered at the time and I still do wonder if it was a confirmation from God that I belonged in that class and that He was with me through my questions, my confusion and my experiences.

I was deeply struck by an article I read in May of that same year. The author said "Our tendency to misunderstand the word, myth, runs parallel with our tendency to misunderstand the word, truth, - which once meant a compact or agreement among things…" (6). In the end, I realized that it was possible for me to understand the Exodus as an ageless truth, a covenant (7) between God and His people.

That same month I read two reviews which were very thought-provoking. Often I read reviews of books that interest me, especially when I think I won't have a chance to read the book.

The first review was on "What is Judaism? An Interpretation for the Present Age" by Emil Fackenheim (8). He said that the Holocaust was, for many, "a primary symbol of Judaism." The reviewer said, "Fackenheim is reticent about discussing the religious issues connected with Israel's occupation of the West Bank, an occupation that, after all, is spearheaded by orthodox settlers who believe that their right to the West Bank is sanctioned by biblical promises."

I found myself saying, "Wait a minute - Judaism has to be about more than the Holocaust and a piece of land - no matter what the piece of land. Where is God in all of that?"

The second review was on the book "God Land - Reflection on Religion and Nationalism" by Conor Cruise O'Brien (9). O'Brien said that the cultures of Israel, South Africa and Ulster "… share a common ideology based on the Old Testament…

God is understood as having given a specific piece of land to a chosen people. …But, he argues, the historical Jesus complicates matters for He preached that His Kingdom was not of this world. Thus, Jesus rejected Old Testament-style nationalism. But when Christianity became the official religion of the late Roman Empire, it became tied to territoriality…"

Questions. So many questions.

"...He touches my arm
And says
Walk with Me
Please..."

Chapter Seven

During the summer of 1988 I decided to take five days alone
at the same Retreat House where I had the dream in 1986
(Chapter Five). The place was almost empty and I kept to myself
completely so it was a time of deep peace and total silence.

I had been looking forward to some quiet time in the Chapel
with my mind still and open but, as usually happens, my mind
was filled with all kinds of nothing and I became increasingly
frustrated. Then as I stood to leave the Chapel I became aware
of the thought "Jesus is tired".

Sometimes one sentence, or two or three words, will pass
through my thoughts. When that happens I put the words on
paper and I wait. Sometimes the rest of the poem flows instantly.
I write quickly, easily and almost without thought. When I've
finished I read the poem over slowly and only then do I fully
grasp its meaning. "Jesus Is Tired" is such a poem. The central

image in this poem is one of a dusty, pale road in the Holy Land. It is really more like a path. On that day in the Chapel I sat down again and wrote these words:

> Jesus is tired
> He withdraws from the crowd
> And passes me
> He touches my arm
> And says
> Walk with Me
> Please
> It's so quiet
> Pebbles rustle slightly underfoot
> I can't believe He asked me
> But He touched my arm
> It wasn't a mistake
> I look at Him
> This is Jesus
> There's so much I want to say
> Should I
> It's probably silly
> What if I …
> And He looks at me
> He smiles
> He knows
> But He needs silence
> His
> Mine

I had been reading a book which mentioned mantras, *Love - A Guide for Prayer* (10). The suggestion of having a comfortable mantra and a beautiful quiet spot for the mind to go was very appealing so I decided that I would have to try that at some time. But what had a far greater impact on me than the mantra concept was the book's talk of the power of God. I realized that I had never thought about the power of God and that, at some level, I was very frightened by this "power", because all of my experiences of God were happening within me. In the stillness and solitude of the Retreat House setting I had time to reflect on my experiences over the previous three years. I realized that I had not tried to deal with any of them. I had not tried to analyze them or myself at the time they happened.

As I thought about the first experience, I realized that if I truly believed the last line **"I WILL ALWAYS BE WITH YOU"** I could handle or finally be rid of any fear. That I have been given much was not in question. In fact, these days on my private retreat were a time of deep awareness and appreciation of the countless gifts in my life.

So I was at the line **"I AM ASKING MUCH OF YOU."** I realized that in over three years I had never asked the obvious question because I was afraid of the answer.

In a kind of conversation with God as I walked on the beach I asked Him what it was that He wanted me to do. I found it extremely difficult to ask that question because I was sure that it would be answered and that really frightened me. Since all of my experiences had happened within me or had been so powerful that they resulted in changes within me, I was sure that pattern would continue. There is no escaping an internal experience. I had no idea what God would ask of me but I knew I would be facing the answer within my own mind. In the background of my thoughts my imagination was running amok. Could my task be to endure horrible physical pain or death like the martyrs, or maybe live out my life like a saint? I knew I was incapable of all of those things. My fear was deep, almost visceral. It seemed to involve my total being. I tried to talk to God about this kind of fear and I asked to be given the courage to understand and accept His answer.

As I returned to the Retreat House through a very lush and beautiful path filled with ferns and trees and wild flowers, I was overwhelmed by the beauty of the scene. I decided to use that image and the mantra **"I WILL ALWAYS BE WITH YOU"** so I began that quiet repetition as I walked. I thought that the mantra was probably too long and that I should be sitting still but I tried it anyway.

It was getting dark but I carried on to the Chapel to spend a little quiet time before bed. Knowing my fear of being alone in darkness and what my fear does to my imagination, I thought maybe I'd be better off going to my room. But, in the end I decided to go to the Chapel because the Chapel was beautiful in the evening. Also, I remembered that I had managed to spend time there on earlier evenings. But this night was different.

I had just asked God a question - an extended question - that was frightening for me: "What are You asking of me? What is the 'much' that You are asking of me?" I continued to feel a deep fear because I was afraid of how He might answer and what He might say. I closed my eyes to calm and focus my mind by picturing the path in the woods. But something was happening. The path was beginning to change shape.

I opened my eyes to feel safe again - rooted and connected to my surroundings. Twilight filled the Chapel with a soft amber glow. The only other light was the candle burning beside the Tabernacle. The beauty and serenity calmed me. So I closed my eyes again and pictured the dusty, pale road of the poem "Jesus Is Tired". But the image was changing and moving. It was frightening to me. I would open my eyes, look around the Chapel and hope that when I closed them again the path would look normal to me, but that did not happen. I think I had started to cry and I know I was going to leave but I remembered reading about fear being the greatest tool of the devil, in *Love - A Guide For Prayer* (10). At that I thought that if God had something to say to me it would probably come in the form of images, and maybe the devil, or whatever evil is, didn't want me to see. So I prayed desperately for courage and I stayed.

When I closed my eyes again the image was of the lush green path, but two objects - something yellow and something black - came tumbling and crashing out of the woods and onto the path, which was changing shape. The objects were huge carton-like shapes that appeared to be fighting. Finally they were in the picture alone and changing sizes and positions constantly. Then the yellow part became very firm and long and tall like a straight wall. This wall seemed to be in three parts which came together as one, seamlessly. The black part took the shape of huge, thick black tongs, which seemed as long as the wall was high. They were shaped like the kitchen tongs we use to pick up something hot but they were thickly padded all over. It looked like the kind of soft foam padding one finds on earphones. They kept opening and closing but couldn't grasp anything.

Then I became aware that someone, a man, frightening and evil looking, was standing off to the side and staring - directly at me. He was clearly a man but something about his face and beard reminded me of a cat. He was holding onto a thin, tall round post with his right hand. Our focus on each other seemed like a long, staring stand-off while we waited for a victor in the fight mentioned above. I have never in my life seen such a look of deadly malice but I somehow sensed that we both knew he couldn't touch me until the fight was over and only then if he won. At the time, I also remember thinking that he could rip out a person's heart or gouge out his eyes without compunction.

Then it looked as if this man were standing on the side of a boat although I didn't see the boat. He seemed to be halfway between the black and yellow image and another image of white, pure white, with shapes on the sides which I cannot describe accurately because I don't remember them well. I think the middle portion of both sides was recessed. The white section looked as if it might lead to a lower level of a small boat. I think it was then that I recognized that whiteness as the inside of a casket!

Suddenly something snapped down hard. I understood that to have happened. Although I didn't see anything snap down I was aware of it and I then became aware of something speeding across the water. It was night. As I looked at the back of the "boat" I realized that it looked like a sealed coffin. As the imagery ended I remember hoping that this experience might mean the death in me of something that was supposed to die.

As I continued to sit with my eyes closed, the path through the woods kept turning sideways. It was still green and leafy but it seemed to be taking firm shape, like a long wooden beam. It looked suspiciously like part of a Cross. I tried desperately to visualize the path as it was in reality.

That image ended but a new one took its place. I could see a Cross of gray set against nothing. Jesus was hanging from it.

He was gray also. He was dead. His head hung down in front of His left shoulder. But the Cross was in a state of flux, disappearing from the bottom up into a huge mass of something gray. I thought the mass was people. The gray mass was almost up to His waist when it dropped back. As the lower part of the Cross became visible again I could see that it was twisted and distorted - pulled to one side.

I opened my eyes and looked at the Tabernacle and the Cross in the Chapel. Then I closed my eyes. As I did so I saw again the mental image of the dead body of Jesus on the Cross. As often happens, one image replaced another. It simply occurred, and I saw a different image. I now saw that someone was holding onto the crossbeam over the right arm of Jesus, whose body colour was now normal. She was supporting herself by hooking the crossbeam under her left arm and wrapping her arm and hand tightly around it. I knew I was that person. Then I was looking down from that perspective and kicking down with my right foot, pushing people off the Cross. (That action is so out of character for me that I must have felt desperately that Jesus was in danger. Yet He was already dead. I don't understand but I do remember feeling that He needed my protection against the aggressive mob.)

Another seamless change of imagery and I was facing the Cross and could see that it was perfectly straight but surrounded at the base by the gray mass. The body of Jesus and the Cross were in natural colour. I am not sure whether it was at this moment or when I was on the Cross looking down, but I have written in my notes from that time that I thought the people were moaning but I wasn't sure.

I struggled to find peace in my other image of walking on

the road with Jesus but everything had changed. It looked like the same area but I'm not sure it was the same road. Someone was on the ground with his chest elevated by his arms. He was staring straight ahead. It seemed that he was being pulled backward as if maybe he were disappearing from the feet up, too. His face didn't show much reaction of any kind and he didn't seem to know or care that I was there.

He looked different, not like Jesus, my companion, on the road in the poem. He was older. I think he wore a King's crown. When I saw what was happening to him I was confused. I'm not sure I knew him but I knew his name. It was "Christ".

As soon as I had that thought, something in the mental image came racing through the air toward my head. The object was dark, very unlike the rest of the image, which was pale, and it was threatening. It was in front of my forehead and beside my head but not touching me. I put up my arm to protect myself.

I opened my eyes and I was crying. I decided to go to bed and begged to be allowed to sleep without nightmares.

My prayers were answered. The following morning as I walked along the beach I had a thought which shocked me. I wondered if it were a crown of thorns that had been racing toward my head in the previous night's image.

I assume that the black part of the struggle was my fear, which was huge and had to be dealt with. Maybe this was my own personal demon.

As for the rest, I have never studied it in any detail since it happened. Whenever my thoughts head in that direction, they veer off somewhere or simply dissolve along the way. I know it happened and I understand the general theme but, for some reason, the whole experience rests very lightly in my memory and my thoughts.

"...I recognize Your presence
In the light of possibilities
Open
Boundless
Waiting for me..."

Chapter Eight

In July of either 1988 or 1989, I was given a book by the same friend who had told me the story of the elderly man in 1986 (Chapter Three). When she handed it to me she said, "It's funny but I can't remember where or when I bought this book." She said she thought I'd enjoy it because I seemed to enjoy the story. Later, reading it alone, I knew half-way down the first page that this was the story of my experience of expanded consciousness. When I saw the words "old man" I knew there would also be a dog and a window box. That's all I remembered but I was absolutely thrilled to see those words appear. The book was *The Greatest Miracle in the World* by Og Mandino (11).

Although I was sure that this was the story my friend had told me, I wanted to verify that fact with her. I reminded her of where and when I had first heard the story from her and she said that was correct.

When I read the book I somehow believed that the words of the book were written for me, personally. It is a wonderful story about how we are responsible for limiting ourselves and how capable we are of returning from a "living death" to realize our full potential.

After reading the book I had a short-lived but truly remarkable sense of confidence that I could do anything. I was thrilled to be alive. It seemed no goal was too lofty. Actually, I talked very seriously with others about starting one of several new businesses but, as life unfolded, new responsibilities intervened. It is also true and perhaps more accurate to say that I couldn't make the business ideas work at that time. Also, I had only a partial understanding of this new "something-to-do" in my mind - something about a business but not at that time and not the kind I was considering. That glimmer of an idea that takes time to understand fully is a much more familiar experience now.

Also, I quickly realized that the words of the Mandino book, while meant for me, were also meant for every other reader. I was embarrassed to think that I had ever felt otherwise.

The book calls for reading a chapter entitled "The God Memorandum" every night before bed for one hundred nights - without exception. Although I believe in both the words and the effect they would have, I have never accomplished that task. I have started in earnest many times but I have yet to make it to ten consecutive nights, never mind one hundred.

Another very meaningful book I read, *A Course in Miracles* (12) says: "Few appreciate the real power of the mind . . . It never sleeps. Every instant it is creating." Og Mandino's book says, ". . . and then sleep in peace, while the message you have read gradually seeps down into your deep mind that never sleeps."

I know that we must undo the errors in our thinking in order to remove the obstacles which block our awareness of the truth. I believe the one hundred day exercise with "The God Memorandum" would be a valuable means of assisting that process.

Given the way *The Greatest Miracle in the World* entered my life it may have real significance for me so I will persevere in my efforts to complete the one hundred days.

* * *

In 1998, I finally finished reading "The God Memorandum" for one hundred consecutive nights. Toward the end I missed two or three nights but tried to focus on the four underlying principles of this text for a few minutes when that happened.

I should add that I was often inattentive, tired and distracted as I read, but that lessened as time passed. What was constant was my desire to read and absorb the words each time I started.

I don't know if or how my experiences were connected to the book but what happened in my life during the same time period was truly amazing. I completed "By Invitation Only". Big decisions were made - easily. Sometimes solutions to problems appeared from external circumstances. Everything seemed to "dove-tail" into place.

Now, at the end of the one hundred days, I look at my life with astonishment and delight. Issues surrounding housing, family, finances, future plans and personal aspects of my life have all changed - many dramatically - and all for the better. I don't remember consciously applying the guidelines of Og Mandino's book very often in daily living but maybe I was working with or flowing with the possibilities of my life in a new way. It's not that life is problem-free now but I seem to be living it from a new and exciting perspective. I have a quiet confidence in my ability, which is a most welcome gift.

"...All my touchstones
All falling away
With each passing I panic
Grieve the loss
Then slowly feel new ground beneath me..."

Chapter Nine

Within a period of three or four days in 1989 I was asked a serious question about faith by two people for whom I have great respect. I wanted to give an answer worthy of the question but, instead, I seemed to give a rather feeble reply. That started me thinking about what my experience of faith had been. I wrote the following essay for my own use several days later.

On Faith

At a time in my life when I couldn't seem to find anything that was honest and true and real, when I felt I was making a complete mess of my life (although the opposite appeared to be true) I began to eliminate from my mind those things which couldn't stand the test of my scrutiny. I knew I had to do something about my life very soon but I didn't know what. At this time I was seeking, almost desperately, something that I could know as a rock-solid truth - a starting point - something on which I could build. What started out as a conscious examination of my faith seemed more an instinctive turning toward God. My faith seemed vague, loose and unrelated to "religion" as I was hearing it explained - but I knew there was something "right" about it.

As I started down this path of turning toward God it was as often uncomfortable and wrong-feeling as it was gentle and soothing. Very quickly I seemed to come to a point of choice no matter how I tried to avoid it. Clearly I saw two different ways my life could be directed. I could fumble along trying to sort things out myself or I could give up control and trust God.

I realized I didn't know God very well; yet it was crystal clear that we couldn't both be directing my life. The paths were too different. I wanted to deal in concrete reality and I sensed I was being offered something very different - something based on trust and patience - determined in God's time, not mine. As I understood that I was moving toward a conscious decision to trust God more, and my instincts and impatience less, my thoughts filled with old negative feelings about holiness. At some time I had come to associate piety and saintliness with an unhappy lifestyle. If I embraced this "holy life" I feared it might result in embracing poverty, sacrifice and isolation. I recoiled from that unappealing vision for my life. Yet I kept seeking that love, that protective hug, that made me feel safe - that told me everything would be alright.

Then, without a conscious crossing-over point, something wonderful began to happen. I had been dealing with a concept of God who was "out there somewhere", and in conversational prayer I still was, but what changed was very much within me - very real. My daily life was exactly the same but my understanding of it was clearing. Looking at problem situations very familiar to me I began to see them in a new way. Like a picture coming into an ever-clearer focus, I began to hear, to know, to understand, the pain or the fear or the innocence in a comment - to understand what wasn't being said and where the comment was coming from. Now, when I responded, I was able to come from this new "place", this new perspective.

As time passed I realized that Love, capital "L", unconditional love, seemed to be the answer over and over. Finally I began to trust in love as the solution, having experienced miraculous results - to see it as my rock of truth. It was in the wisdom of that love that I could find my answers. Love became as real a truth for me as the tables and chairs I could touch. My faith was not drawing me out to some heavenly future but it was gently inviting me inward, into my present self. Although this was my personal journey I sensed I would be protected as I walked this unfamiliar terrain of searching and trusting.

Often, after a strong dream or the painful recognition of some dark area within myself, I would feel, emotionally, like putting my hands over my head to protect myself because something awful was coming. But that never happened. Everything I came to understand was something I could be comfortable with, something I could know as true once I made the right connection. And then the struggle was over. It slipped past me as history, not some buried, living hurt that continued to inflict pain. Slowly I began to understand that this spiritual part of me - my personal, unique spirit - was as much a living part of me as my flesh and bones were. Not only that, it was the centre of everything I was.

This same journey, this journey into my centre, into who I am, is a journey toward God - straight to Him. The more I understand of myself, the more I understand of God.

"...Clearly
Your invitation to love
Calls for personal responsibility
Promises Your wisdom
Guarantees the power of love..."

Chapter Ten

At the end of June 1989 my husband and I were asked to provide our input about the formation of priests by answering a specific question. We thought that both the issue and the approach were important so we were happy to participate along with many other lay people.

Our question was as follows:

"A totally integrated formation: application of the Ratio Institutionis -

"Some episcopal conferences have established a Ratio Studiorum, others work to its editing or its revision. In reference to the Ratio Fundamentalis, is the application of these norms in conformity with the directives of Roman authority and to those given by the Bishops? In particular, in the framework of an integral formation, does the system of study thus established ensure the preparation of pastors capable of understanding their times, of announcing the gospel to the people of today and of leading others to an apostolic faith in communion and in fidelity to the ordinary magisterium of the Sovereign Pontiff and of bishops? What problems are posed in relation to this subject?"

No matter how many times I read the question, I couldn't seem to get past the language or to formulate any kind of an answer. My husband and I had agreed that whichever one of us felt able to respond, he or she would do so, check it over with the other and then mail it in before the August 15th deadline. Almost four weeks had passed by the time I had this experience:

One night I woke up about three and couldn't get back to sleep. I got up and walked into the livingroom. At that point I decided to answer the Bishop's question.

I wrote the letter which follows from start to finish without hesitating once. Then I went back to bed and slept soundly. In the morning I read the letter again, checked it out with my husband, wrote a good copy and mailed it.

This letter is one of many examples of the paradox I referred to earlier which is the combination of intimate involvement and yet detachment within the same work. I wrote the words. I recognized the thoughts as mine; yet the words of the letter seemed to flow through me more then come from my mind. I had no idea what was coming next.

If I were writing this letter today I would change two sentences which continue to bother me. I said, "...I do believe in the possibility of working through every crisis. With God's help we are able to achieve a deep and satisfying life-time commitment whether between a man or woman and God in the priesthood and religious life, or between a man and woman in marriage." I overstated what I know to be true. What I know is that those words were true for me. I have no idea if they're true for everyone else.

25 July 1989

Dear Bishop:

Thank you for allowing us to participate in the dialogue which precedes your Synod of Bishops in 1990. I think that is a wise and courageous action.

I have read the questions regarding the formation of priests several times but I cannot seem to address the specific questions by themselves.

Please allow me to respond in the only way that I am able. I do so humbly, respectfully and lovingly from within the family of the Church. I hope you will find my comments relevant and helpful.

It seems to me that we often act, as a Church, from a place of misunderstanding and fear. We come from the perspective of history and tradition first and I think that is very risky. It is difficult enough to see the truth of the present without filtering it through the perceptions of people who have lived in the last 2000 years but who are now dead. They responded to their faith, their culture, the problems of their time as they chose and I respect that. I am not in the least judgmental because I do not know or understand the circumstances of their lives.

If we are to be truthful I think that we must recognize also that many of our traditions are questionable. We find their roots in power, in an alliance of Church with State. Is it not true that the magnificent robes date back to Kings and Emperors not to Christ? How can we be a Church with a preferential option for the poor, a Church which demonstrates the transforming power of love when we align ourselves in any way with wealth and not with poverty and suffering? It is how we live and act and not what we say which touches people.

I understand, at least somewhat, our history and traditions but I feel that I owe no allegiance to either. I cannot. Everything I have come to understand up to this point in my life tells me otherwise. I think that the purpose, the challenge of my life is to live through each moment using Christ as my only role model. In our short years of mature spirituality I believe that is what we are all called to do - to focus on the present through Christ's eyes and then to act clearly, directly and decisively with Him and through Him.

We worry about decreasing vocations but I think we are missing something. Everything I read in the Gospels about Jesus tells me that people, by the thousands, loved Him dearly. They wanted to be close to Him, to listen to Him, to touch Him, to follow Him, so much so that He frequently had to retreat from them for quiet moments alone. He was a very appealing person. This is the truth of the situation. We are as spiritual as we are physical and emotional. If Christ is a living God, and He is, the same situation exists today. Seeing Him, sensing His presence touches a part of every one of us that is alive and real. We instinctively want to respond - and we will. Could that be one of our problems today? Somehow, in spite of all the goodness and wisdom and holiness existing within the Church, Christ is not being seen or felt and consequently people are not following Him.

I wonder if we have distorted some other basic ideas too. It seems to me that we have misunderstood what is being asked of us by God. We have seen our personal needs and desires as signs of weakness and sinfulness to be denied so that we might serve God better. I think the exact opposite is true. We must come to know ourselves deeply and to accept our strengths and weaknesses before we can have a deep and meaningful relationship with the God who created us as we are. Part of who we are is our very powerful and beautiful human sexuality. It is difficult, I believe, to place and keep that in the healthy perspective God intended. To understand all of these personal forces within and then to offer them to God for a lifetime is a gift of incredible magnitude. I doubt that all who wish to dedicate their lives to God's service are capable of such a gift.

I do know the power of the Sacraments and I do believe in the possibility of working through every crisis. With God's help we are able to achieve a deep and satisfying lifetime commitment, whether between a man or woman and God in the priesthood and religious life or between a man and woman in marriage.

Finally, in searching for answers to our many serious problems, I do not understand how or why the Catholic Church denies the very gifts of the Spirit for which we pray. Surely, our living God is revealing and will continue to reveal Himself through the gift of wisdom which He promised. Maybe these revelations will be challenging and frightening but they are essential nonetheless. It seems a grave error to attempt to dictate the parameters of Catholic thought, to say nothing of the fact that it is impossible.

Recently, I returned from my hometown of Windsor, Ontario, very upset about the closure of so many inner-city Churches across the river in Detroit. In discussing it with my husband he said something which had the distinct ring and clarity of truth. I think we must always be open to wisdom and truth from whatever source. He said, "They are closing the wrong Churches. What a beautiful opportunity to really exercise the preferential option for the poor! The suburban Churches should be closed and those people who have cars for transportation could then come to the inner-city Churches and share their love, faith, money and commitment. Working side by side with the poor would be a real celebration of Eucharist."

The comments I have made may sound naive and simplistic but I hope that they are neither.

I cannot imagine how complicated it must be to live with the responsibilities of being a Bishop. My husband and I have been deeply moved by the loving guidance and wisdom of past statements from the Bishops of Canada. I will pray for all of you when you meet at this very painful time in the Canadian Catholic Church.

Respectfully yours,

Gail Higgins.

My need to correct this letter is an excellent example of how this book came together. When I made an error in accuracy, it would return to my mind again and again until I corrected the problem. It has been impossible for me to write anything that is not the exact truth as I understand it. This letter would have followed that pattern had I not mailed it within hours of writing it.

"...Your Light
Fills me
Shines through me
Becomes me..."

Chapter Eleven

One morning in the spring of 1990 I was sitting in front of the Tabernacle after a weekday Mass. It was very peaceful and quiet. I think I was alone in the church, my eyes closed. Then clearly, in my mind, I saw a body split in half and opened like a shell. I recognized that it was my body. I was seeing it from a short distance back and looking at it from the top of the head down. The centre of my body was filled with a beautiful light which was one with a ray of light from above. Somehow I understood clearly that my body was not being suffused with light. It *was* light - the one, same light.

I don't know if it was then or when I opened my eyes that I had a complete awareness of the irrelevance of my body. It felt wonderful - liberating. I had a complete awareness of my oneness with God. When I opened my eyes I was amazed to find that my face was tilted upward and my palms were facing up and resting on my knees. I was breathing in a way that is difficult to describe. It was slow and deep beyond words - as if my lungs were completely emptying and then filling to absolute capacity. I felt that every breath was a head to toe experience. Almost instantly I realized that I had to correct my breathing because I didn't know how to breathe in that manner. It was like an instant of respiratory panic. It took five or six breaths to come back to what felt normal, but so very shallow.

"...Somewhere I am
Still
Certain
Waiting..."

Chapter Twelve

The following dream experience happened in the spring of 1990. I seemed to understand the entire dream when I opened my eyes and I felt calm and peaceful. That was a different experience from the earlier dream in 1986 (Chapter Five). The fact that I understood it seemed strange also. It seemed to be a remarkable visual summary of my spiritual journey to that point and I recognized it as accurate. I have included it here because it seems to connect directly to a poem I wrote in 1995. This poem is very important to me. It expresses my truth. It is how I survive. As always, I can only hope that my understanding, my presentation and my inclusion of events are as they should be.

Some part of me understands
Somewhere I am
Still
Certain
Waiting
Like the cook with his cleaver
I follow the Spirit
Along the natural line
Through the hidden spaces
The secret openings
I know nothing of

When I reread the first five lines in 1995 I was surprised and confused because my life felt chaotic and stressful. Then I remembered my 1990 dream and I knew that there was, indeed, such a place within me.

In this poem I paraphrased the words of another to express my own thoughts. The words come from *The Way of Chuang Tzu* (13). I find Merton's interpretations of the work of this great Taoist philosopher inspiring and compelling but it was only when I read "Cutting Up an Ox" that I recognized a personal truth in the lines about the Spirit. I have placed these in brackets. I *knew* these words. I had lived them.

Cutting Up An Ox

... "When I first began
     To cut up oxen
     I would see before me
     The whole ox
     All in one mass.

"After three years
I no longer saw this mass.
I saw the distinctions.

"But now, I see nothing
with the eye. My whole being apprehends.
(My senses are idle. The spirit
free to work without plan
Follows its own instinct
Guided by natural line,
By the secret opening, the hidden space,)

… ("There are spaces in the joints;
    The blade is thin and keen:
    When this thinness
    Finds that space
    There is all the room you need!)

… ("True, there are sometimes
    tough joints. I feel them coming,
    I slow down, I watch closely,
    Hold back, barely move the blade…)

My brother-in-law passed along two books which affected me deeply. Merton's book was one. The other was called "The Grand Inquisitor" (14). It is part of *The Brothers Karamazov* but has been published separately. It struck me as one of the most thought-provoking and challenging pieces of spiritual reading that I have ever done. Over the years I have read it a number of times, always with the same reaction.

What follows is the dream experience of 1990:

The Dream

I was driving toward a hospital parking garage. I knew everything was huge. I guess that meant the hospital and the car park. I was aware that I knew people in other cars who were heading in the same direction. These people mattered very much to me - at least some of them did. They felt like my family. I tried to look through my windshield but I couldn't see because it was completely fogged up. I tried to wipe it clean but I couldn't. The fog was on the outside so I couldn't drive.

Then, somehow, my car was in the garage and I was near the entrance on the first floor looking around to find it. I was already inside. I was confused and overwhelmed. That made it rather frightening for me. It was huge and noisy and busy - like a foundry maybe as well as a car park.

A man in a three-piece suit walked past me at a brisk clip. He had a briefcase and seemed to know exactly where his car was. I didn't have any idea at all where to go or what to do.

Something - just to the right and in front of me - was leading upward but it wasn't a staircase. It was like a chute or half of a big pipe that was flatish on the bottom. I jumped on and tried to climb but I was aware that some huge moving part (like an automated machine) was going to come swinging in behind me. At that moment I knew I'd be killed so I jumped off. The swinging part fitted the pipe and would clear out everything in its path, but it didn't fit the pipe snugly. It would have been possible to stay on the left and survive and climb but it would have been very hard to do. How would you climb that kind of surface and not fall backward? There was a getting off point though. The pipe only went as high as the second floor, which I could see from where I was.

Then I was standing alone around the corner from the front entrance. I was still on the first floor and I was looking all around and looking up. I was totally overwhelmed by my surroundings and my confusion. It was impossible for me to find my way. I knew my husband was up there somewhere so I called his name several times. He came to the railing immediately. I could see him clearly but he was very high. I don't remember words but I remember understanding him to say, "It's alright. Don't worry. I'm coming for you right now." I was amazed that he didn't think my helplessness was foolish or a bother. He wasn't surprised to see me but his face seemed to show more of a look of concern than happiness.

Then I was standing in front of the down escalator. The one beside it was going up. I was waiting for him to come and get me. I knew for sure that he was on his way. Suddenly I understood what was wrong with me. This garage that other people understood was an impossible maze for me! I couldn't find my car. I couldn't understand the layout. In fact, my helplessness was so total that I couldn't do anything. I couldn't move without being led. I just stood there - quietly - waiting.

Upon awakening I realized that I had never experienced the totality, the absoluteness of that feeling of helplessness at any other time in my life. Also, I understood that when I was heading toward "the hospital" of this dream, I was heading toward the place of healing, toward God. I was sure that my calls for my husband in the dream were calls for God who would rescue me. I knew I could trust Him. I knew He would come for me.

I recognize that there are contradictions between some of the threatening dream imagery and my feeling of deep peace upon awakening. I think the dream used strong images to show me truths that were absolute for me. It was impossible for me to think my way through my confusion. I believe my deep sense of peace came from the certainty of knowing that I was in God's hands and I was safe. It seemed to be a passing over of trust from myself to God.

"This day hasn't happened
The possibilities are staggering"

Chapter Thirteen

Maybe four or five times over the last ten years I have had a brief but thrilling experience that feels like an instant of being fully alive - of living up to the possibilities of the moment. Everything becomes so vibrant and clear that words like fun, laughter and physical feel like they should be part of the description. I understand other people, myself, the weather, my surroundings, everything, in a new way. I am not an observer. I am aware of and actively participating in the wonder of this moment. It's like a wonderful, natural high. It would be an incredible way to live through the days of life - one moment at a time. Without limits everything and anything seem possible. Although I'm sorry when these brief and fleeting moments end, I always feel that it's almost within my power to return to that "space", but I have yet to make it back there on my own.

"...Almost
An aching call of
Remember Me
Remember that you know Me..."

Chapter Fourteen

In September of 1990 I read a book review in the "Catholic New Times" on *A Course in Miracles* (15). The reviewer began by saying, "Never have I read anything remotely like this astonishing and compelling book." The review described the actions of a research psychologist at Columbia University Medical Center in 1965. Helen Shucman was a woman in her mid 50's, "an atheist and a Jew with no religious upbringing." She "began mentally 'hearing' a voice" which asked her to "take notes." Fearing for her sanity, she confided in the Director of her Department. Although he was an agnostic, he urged her to continue recording her thoughts. For seven years, she took "this dictation in short-hand" and the Director typed it out the next day.

The review stated, "The aim of the book is not to elicit doctrinal belief but to bring about spiritual awakening, which is the primary 'miracle' of its title."

The review concluded by saying that because the book which resulted, *A Course in Miracles*, "has never been promoted, sent out for review or advertised, it remains relatively unknown."

Under any circumstances, those comments alone would have deeply intrigued me but that is not what compelled me to find and read this book. When I read that Helen Shucman "began mentally 'hearing' a voice" I knew I had to read more about her experience. It had been over five years since I had mentally 'heard' those first three sentences:

"I AM ASKING MUCH OF YOU

I HAVE GIVEN YOU MUCH

I WILL ALWAYS BE WITH YOU"

In all that time I had not read or heard of anything that connected to my experience of understanding those sentences - until this review of *A Course in Miracles*. I was profoundly affected by this book. I know that many of us are suspicious of new religious ideas but these are not new. They are a clarification. There were a few ideas I had difficulty getting my mind around but as the preface said, I didn't reject them. I just let them be.

A Course in Miracles, for me, is not about any 'formal' religion or even about being religious but it is about the sacredness of life. I found it to be a joyous, liberating and healing book about the experience and the possibility of relationships - with each other and with our Creator.

Section Two

Poems

"...A space of deep connection
To an unknown now
Where I am present
Able to draw on its depth..."

The Poems

The act of writing feels like a deep and gentle search - a movement through the known and unknown spaces of my mind to seek out the exact truth of that moment of intense experience. The words become, somehow, an extension of my mind - a place where the loose ends are pulled together - sometimes a place of questions, sometimes a place of answers.

I thank God with a depth He understands for giving me someplace to go that releases and expands my thoughts. The poems are my stepping stones to greater understanding. When I read the words I recognize what I know.

The similarity of some poems may be best explained by the comments of a wise and knowledgeable friend. She said, "There are only so many areas one touches on in a spiritual search but, over time, we pass them again and again in an ever-deepening spiral. With each encounter we may see and understand the meaning in a slightly different way."

*   *   *

Since this is my first experience of writing poetry I'll explain how it happened.

We had just started our summer vacation in 1985. It was very early in the morning and I was sitting up in bed sipping a coffee. I remember enjoying the beauty of the day and my surroundings immensely.

Our summer camp or cottage is a great treasure in our lives. It has a rich and wonderful history as well. The richness of this history may have been in my thoughts somewhere because it is part of a poem that follows.

As I sipped my coffee, I became aware of a strong urge to write something down so I reached for the notepad I always kept close at hand. With the ease and speed of a newsy letter I wrote without hesitation or correction. I finished with a title.

When I looked at what I had written I was amazed and delighted. I felt I had just done the first truly creative thing of my life. I was so busy enjoying the fact that it had happened that I didn't stop to wonder about the why or how.

It looked like a poem to me but I wondered if I could dare to call it one. I told myself that if it was a poem then I was a poet. I played with that thought so much that I could almost see my destiny unfolding brilliantly. I even had the gall to mention to my sister-in-law, ever-so-casually, that I had been writing poetry, to feel the rush of saying it out loud - just once.

I tried many times to write again, without success. Finally I stopped trying. I told myself it was some kind of fluke, a one-time experience.

I don't remember, nor has it ever mattered, whether I wrote a poem at the moment a particular thought occurred or later. The moment always seemed locked into memory. Experiences happened and life went on. Aside from keeping the poems in chronological order, there was no cross-referencing of one experience with another. As time passed, I could never gauge the reaction of anyone who read what I had written nor could I overcome my self-consciousness. Although the first poem did not strike me as God-centered at the time, I realized quickly that "religious" words or writings often cause people's eyes to glaze over - including my own. So, for the most part, my poetry became a private and treasured collection of my experiences.

Moments in Time (1985)

i
Wise old trees
        Soft waves lapping
        God's creatures abound
History unfolds
        Repeats
Fulfilled
        Complete

ii
Music
        Laughter
        Splashing
Human life
Riverboats
Muffled voices
Tinkling glasses
Bouncing balls

Water games
      Giggles
      Shouts
No war here
      No depression
Pink twilights
Floating chiffon
Skipping rocks
Eternal love
   Until the whistle blows

            iii
Wise old trees
      Soft waves lapping
Only God's creatures break the silence

            iv
Babies crying
      Squealing
Tiny toes curl
      Cool water tickles them
Old records
   Warm memories
         Stories shared
               Treasured
Of Ray and Walter
Of eels
   Caps on telephones
Dauntless fishermen
   Loyalist roots
   Glamourless lives

v

The phone
   The car
Broken hearts
Life stops
   A precious heart struggles
God smiles
A gift of sorts
   Never forgotten
Everything deepens
   Joy
   Pain
Eyes clearer
   Hearing sharper
Lives
   Life
More precious

vi

Raucous ball games
   Food for the soul
   Gales of laughter
Being there counts
Rules bend
   Hearts grow
Everyone wins

vii

Bulldozers
   History moves
Logs and strong backs
Erosion
   Poplar groves

Lighthouse
Yes
    Here
We choose here

    viii
Nature decorates
    Memory is short
The camp and land are one again
Hammers
    Sweat
A surgeon's brain
    And a carpenter's soul
Justifiable pride
    Luxury now
    No needs unmet

    ix
New voices
    New visions
Loving patience
    Appreciation
The land thrives
    Blossoms
The camp sparkles
    Grows
    Deepens
    Glows
The camp
The land
Our lives
    Are one
More sunsets seen

Crackling ball games
Cigarettes and black flies
No war here
   No depression

          x
Curled toes in Adidas sneakers
Warm milk in brown bottles
Old records on the Top 10
Baby boys have broad shoulders
Girlfriends
   In sweat suits
      Not chiffon
Young open faces
Young open lives
Sports
Plans
Fears
Loves
Deep
   But passing
Baby girls cherished
   Make-up
   Giggles
Jigsaw puzzles
Each new piece brings them closer to
      completion

          xi
Stop
   Time
Let the sweetness linger

God's Gift - Our Treasure (1985)

She's 13 today
   Sweet
   Loving
   Open
Innocence awaiting life
Eternal optimism
Free to do
   Be
   Anything
Prince Charming exists
'Another World' is another world
Real life means
   Security
   Tenderness
   Love
God protect her loving innocence

Bouncy curls
Smokey hazel eyes
Crooked teeth in a dimpled smile
Pink razors and blue eye-shadow

Do you love me
Am I pretty
Are you proud of me
Urgent unspoken questions
May she hear affirmation in our garbled responses
She held the key that unlocked doors
      Bared treasured gifts of emotion
           Insight
           Depth
           Love

She needs us
      To be sure
We all need unconditional love
      A safe haven

Do we need her
Who would
      Call up our tenderness
      Bake our birthday cakes
      Design our bedroom mobiles
      Shove loving notes under the door
      Plan for holidays two months in advance
      Hug me when I'm down

A tiny gift passed from arm to arm
      One cold November day

How could we ever know
      How priceless this treasure
      How precious this life

*   *   *

This poem arose from feelings of humiliation and failure which, in this instance, were connected to my pride.

The event of that day was a peace conference where I was neither prepared nor peaceful. The day was reasonably successful but I had a well-deserved sense of disappointment in myself.

In the middle of the following night I was feeling very drained emotionally in a general way. The memory of me in a heated argument at a peace conference did not help. The poem flowed from the darkness of that time and mood but, as usual, was not about my superficial feelings.

Everything Is … (1986)

Everything is too much
     Empty
     Faceless
Who am I anyway
Like the sea
     The tides
I rise
     Fall
Advance
     Retreat
Human seagulls pick at my bones
Where is the hope
Drifting
     Wasting
My anchor floats
So hollow

Praise fills me up
Affirmation convinces me
Alone I have no value

Why bother
Empty rewards
The spirit withers
Dies . . .
No
It waits for me
To do what

I am clay
Human potters crush my mold
Formless
Valueless
God
My Potter
Salvage this clay
Show me my value

* * *

Do You Like Balloons? (1986)

This one
So precious
So fragile
As balloons go

Nice to have around
Bright and colourful
If you like balloons

Hard to anchor
Destined to rise
   But not now
Always threatening to drift
   Aimlessly
   Uselessly
A dangerous mixture
   Toxic contents
   Vulnerable skin
So easy to puncture
   Deflate
Invisible eyes within
   Waiting
   Silent
   Hopeful
Unlike other balloons
   Or their owners
But precious only to itself
   And its Creator

Don't you see
This balloon is real
Unique
Not transparent
Not disposable
Please
   Don't let go of the string

*   *   *

On 'Letting Go' (1986)

i

The anguish of indecision
  Haunting
  Exciting
  Frightening
The skin I wear every day
Invisible to onlookers
Sometimes
  Comforting
  Warming
  Nourishing
Sometimes
  Binding
  Threatening
  Suffocating

ii

My soul has a life of its own
  Eyes that flash images to me
My brain connects mysteriously
  Confuses
  Clarifies
  Confuses again
Wholeness escapes me
I am a battleground
  Voluntarily
  Involuntarily
Fog and stumbling blocks
I don't know the rules
Where are the black holes
Where is the light

iii

I grow tired
Restless
Overwhelmed
Is this madness
Depression
Or my lonely desert trek
How far
How long
I sense
Forever

iv

The farther I travel
The deeper the turmoil
Is peace a mirage
Do I know peace
Will I recognize it
Not serenity
Joy
Smiles
But the safe haven of a faithful lover

v

This love
So all encompassing
Exclusive
Demanding
Returned a hundred fold
Known only to lovers
Risk
And receive

Withdraw
    And see only the distant glow

vi
I must be wrong
    Confused
Why the pain
My Prince of Peace
    Where are You
My Saviour
    Creator
    Redeemer
    Father

*   *   *

One day when I walked past my son's experiment with plants for school, I was struck by our similarities to these plants. They seemed to be a perfect example of the lowest and highest possibilities of humanity.

Photosynthesis (1986)

Both seeds planted
Nourished by warmth
    Good soil
All things equal
    But for light
One grows
    But barely
The other thrives

Straining toward the light
To be alive
But to subsist
To be fully alive
Bursting forth
Choose light

*   *   *

This poem started like every other poem and I was very moved by it until, at some point, I lost my connection. Even though the words were for my own private use I lost interest when the actual "words" seemed to become the focus. Later I went back and altered the poem, eliminating parts of it. I think that is the only time I ever did that.

Labour (1986)

The canal
So long
So dark
So uncomfortable
But strangely warm
Involuntary contractions
Forward propulsion
Propulsion
Hardly
Micro-movements maybe
A miracle unfolding nonetheless
Connected by a throbbing cord
To youth

Passions
Illusions
Nourished by praise
Power
Success
Now rejecting ties
Moving toward light
Beyond choosing
Being called forth
To new life

A reality which sees
Not looks

Hears
Not listens
Living in and with and through a new
lifeline
A mystical bridge between love and life
Mother and baby
So alike
Yet so different
How secure the womb
Sheltered from reality
Safe from threat but
Parasitic
New life challenges
Exhilarates
Hurts
Confuses
But it is real
Deep
True

Sheltered from death
Safe from abandonment
     Symbiotic

We announce a birth
     Mine

Unfinished (1986)

The river is flowing to the sea
It has ever been thus
We can take picnics on the shore
     Or hide in the bushes
But it is the only way home

Some choose their means of travel
Some are carried along by the current
And others
     Dear God
     Others get caught in the undertow

The speedboats
     Ah, the speedboats
They are exhilarating for some
     Frightening for others
They whiz along the surface
     Seeing little
     Hearing less
The thrills are intense and fleeting
     A personal high
But don't stop that motor

It tells them they're still alive

So the speedboat races upriver
    Against the current
With two haunting questions
    How much gas
    For how long
And one unfaced truth
    The speedboat will drift back to the sea

A Bee (1986)

A bee
    A distant hammer
    A barking dog
And birds
    So many birds
But no voices
    How sweet the absence
This cove of peace
    Touched gently by the waves
Shaped for viewing
    A moving
    Incredibly beautiful performance
I love it
I love You
Thank You

Clouds (1986)

Clouds
      Black
      Passing
Obscuring the sun
But life-giving
Their contents necessary
      Altering
      Sometimes frightening
Always temporary
The loving healing sun returns
      It was never gone

Ode To An Ant (1986)

Fly
      Ant
Why won't you fly
Why do you have wings anyway
You're too busy working
      Clinging to the ground
Because all the other ants are
Try
      For me
You're stupid and frustrating
Maybe I'll step on you
No
      I won't
Someday you might fly
Me too
Good luck

This Feeling (1986)

This feeling
It makes me breathless
Do You know
Do You have any idea
How beautiful this scene is
How much I'm enjoying Your brilliant work
How thankful I am for Your gifts
The sun setting on the water
The waves lapping at my feet
The wind tossing my hair
The hills fading to deep purple
Even the gulls are respectfully silent
Alone
      With You
      With my joy
I'm so happy
      I love You so much
This feels strangely like the rush of new love
      Which never lasts
What about us
      This
Am I carried away by the sunset
Or being carried away by Your love

* * *

Something was changing. Some moments of awareness felt challenging - maybe even nagging or disruptive.

I had come to cherish the sense of deep peace and calm that I felt in quiet moments alone with God. Often I had chosen the time and setting because I felt such a strong need to be still and quiet - but I did feel that *I* was choosing those moments. Then I began to sense an uneasiness or restlessness in my thoughts from time to time. It was not connected to guilt about spending more time with God or more time in prayer. It was more about an increasing awareness of something vague within me and my response or lack of response to that awareness. It was about activity in some form - something to do or think about or understand, needs to be met somewhere - vague but clearly present nonetheless.

(1986)

What are You doing, God?

Now I believe that those moments which "*I* was choosing", when "I felt such a strong need to be still and quiet", were actually moments of invitation being offered to me by God.

* * *

The Wedge (1986)

Are we in trouble
I try harder
   Too hard
The divide widens
Selfless
   Or selfish
Silent acceptance
   Tolerance
Unkind eyes
Unforgiving ears
Vibrations that rack
Where is the love
Hands are cold
   Self-conscious
A touch is warm
   Penetrating
The love sinking
The like ebbing
Do I care
Do we care
To live a lie
   Is to not live
Insignificant incidents
   Monumental responses

God is love
   Find Him
   Reconnect our souls

It isn't working
Help

Aching Bones (1987)

Aching bones
  Chilly mornings
  Cranky restlessness
I want to find You
  But
  On my terms
Not today
At least not now
I want peace
  Silence
  Calm
Still
  You are here
Aware
  Loving
To search more deeply
  To know You better
Takes time
  Energy
It strains
  And drains
The struggle is hard
  Heavy with depth
  Painful with truth
  Tiring with challenge
Always the paradox
  You turn my life upside down
  Confuse me
  Prod me
  Steal my complacency
So I run from You

To find respite
Inner peace
In Your arms
In Your love
How can it be

Donny (1987)

Donny
        Eileen
        Jack
I want to keep faith with you
Not in memory
        As you were
In reality
        As you are
Free
        Complete
Conscious
Separate
Whole
I sense your place
I miss my darling sons
Include them
        Please

*   *   *

If my burdens cannot be lightened for me, please allow
me to carry them in such a way that I lighten them for others.

Even In You ... (1987)

Even in You I feel restless
        Filled with self-pity
        Angry and resentful
I try
And I know You
Intimately
I want to love You more
        Give You more
But it feels hard
        Heavy
        Constant
Have I chosen problems on all sides
Am I missing some lightness of heart
        Some joy
Or have You chosen to lift me up
        By keeping me down
Giving me only one place that eases and heals
With You
We are one
        We talk
        I feel so sure
But my life is a series of struggles
        Of crosses
It's Lent again
Is that it
No matter

I want to walk with You on Calvary
I will be there
        In all my imperfection
        Especially of attitude

                    *   *   *

On Trust (1987)

I am being led
    And I follow
Sometimes reluctantly
I seem to see clearly
    Things that others do not
Why
Knowing first
Understanding later
How
Am I confused
Do I know these things
Are they for my soul alone
I think not
I can only be here
It doesn't feel good
It feels right

I Search … (1987)

I search for You
      And You say
Why
I am here
      In you
We are one
Focus through Me
      See through My eyes
      Listen through My ears
      Love with My love
Be Eucharist
Share Me

Slowly (1987)

Slowly
      Painfully
      Lovingly
The tree is turned
Imperceptible movements snapping roots
But it thrives
      How
Identical yet different
      Totally
How can the movements be slow
      Yet be
      Mysteriously
      Miraculously
      Quantum leaps

This Place ... (1987)

This place feels lonely
      Confusing
I can't share it with anyone
      But I try
      They try
Regrets all around
      Or worse
All my touchstones
All falling away
With each passing I panic
      Grieve the loss
Then slowly feel new ground beneath me
      Deeper
      Stronger support
But invisible
My senses balk
      Demand recognition
Finally but surely
That sweet harmony untangles the knots
All my solutions found here
      Some chosen
      More given
      All incredible
The gifts outweigh the sacrifices a hundred fold
But the sacrifices are almost more than I can bear
      So I don't
I only wish to
      And it is done

How Did This Happen (1987)

How did this happen
We're both in blindfolds
Wielding lethal weapons
And denying it
Assessing and distributing blame
In every language but the spoken one
Internal bartering
     Trade-offs
     Endless arguments
     With an absent partner
Things need to be said
     Understood
But the wall is so high
     We can't reach over
     Or through
And then
     Miraculously
     It's gone
     Like a bad dream
We feel close
     Safe
     Happy
It feels so good
We're going to be better than ever

And then it happens
     Again
How could he do
     Or say
     Such a thing
 I feel sick

How could I be so foolish
    To let my guard down
But a thought nags
    Maybe I started it
    Did I cut him first
We live in a mine field
I want to lash out
    To say
    God knows
    He deserves it
But that's not what God knows
That's not what I know

He knows we love each other
We know that too
Why can't we remember

(1987)

Dear God,
why me?

I Resent … (1987)

I resent the ripples
The stillness was exquisite
Trees in perfect reflection
Birds and squirrels alone broke the silence
I was a grateful guest
And my soul felt the peace
Until the boat
      The reaction
Silent
      But visible
Continuous
      Unstoppable
Ripples grew into waves
      Moved closer
Broke on the shore
Splashing over dry ground
Now I could hear as well as see the water
Had I gained more than I lost
My powerlessness was frightening
      I could merely observe
Where is my sense of fun
      Of marvel
Always so bloody heavy
Waves make children laugh
The picture comes alive
There is order in movement
I guess I like waves
      Sometimes

On Holiness (1987)

Spirituality compared causes panic
Darkness too often eclipses light
But souls are beyond compare
Rightly so
I live with my shadow
        Because I am human
God lives with my shadow
        Because He made me human
            Loves me human
He strikes a saving balance
Slowly His spirit exposes truth
Destroys my ridiculous misconceptions
Fully living and loving life is my call

... Another Gift (1987)

And yet another gift
        Unearned
        But most welcome
I have less to say
        About more subjects
I defer with respect
        It feels easy
        I feel confident
            Not inadequate
I didn't ask for this
        As always
        You knew
Thank You

Another Mystery (1987)

The pain of confrontation
   With truth
      Sin
      Failure
Is so deep it sickens
My mind fragments
   My stomach knots
   My head aches
   Tears flow
Utter despair
   Beyond coping
   Beyond solving
Finally I say
   Help
   Please
The sun rises
   Birds sing
   I survive
And sense
   A corner turned
   A new perspective
Always the problems are solved
Always in ways unimagined by me
That is a miracle
That is a mystery
   But more
All the anguish of confrontation disappears
   Not diminishes
It is beyond recall
Free to start again
   Move on

No extra baggage
I live among miracles
   And I feel very loved
But very small

Is It A Coincidence (1987)

Is it a coincidence
My arthritis grew with my love for You
At the crippling point
Relief was given
Control
   Not cure
As always
   External
   Internal
We have become friends
We live together
   Respect one another
We connect daily
   To varying degrees
Always it hovers
   Keeping me in line
   Reminding me of days past
It is no longer unwelcome
It is my guardian angel

* * *

As I wrote this poem, particularly the last seven lines, I was aware of writing words that felt very convoluted to me.

Now those words can flow through my thoughts as an expression of something I understand but, at the time, the words were weaving some kind of interdependence that was new to me.

How Much Power ... (1987)

How much power do I have
I have the power of Christ
No less
It exists because I am alive
It is transformed by Eucharist
I am transformed by Eucharist
His power to love
     And mine
     Are one
His power to overcome death
     And mine
     Are one
I become His Body and Blood
I am alive because of God
He is alive in my place in history
In my walk through life
Only if I co-create love with Him
Allow Christ to become man
     Through me
     Again and again

Each time He manifests Himself
Through the miracle of love
And transforms

*   *   *

This experience came during a period of great stress and pain in our marriage. It was overwhelming for me. It was one of the times where my tears flowed freely, almost unconsciously. The depth of emotional connection was beyond what any words could convey.

It was a school day and I remember that I was in the kitchen making spaghetti for supper. My youngest son was there with me listening to a Jim Croce tape. I was deeply struck by Jim's words about "hanging on the lover's Cross". I wanted to make a note about what I was thinking. I remember feeling, at the time, that if I had something to write it should take precedence over everything else. Actually, I recall a sense of obligation, of fulfilling my part of some contract I had made with God. Although the feeling was strong on that day, it's not one that I'm usually aware of in daily living. I sat down at the kitchen table and wrote up to the line "movements of grace." I felt there was something more but I didn't know what until this experience happened:

Something began to move within my mind. It was dark and complex. It seemed to be above me and it filled my whole mind. I couldn't make it out but tears were streaming down my face. I then wrote the lines up to "Cross." I knew an incredible experience of intimacy was taking place in that instant and I was truly overwhelmed by it. I believe we all spend time on the Cross during our lives. But I had never considered this possibility of how Jesus shares our painful experiences with us. The thought that we are not there alone, that we are being gently and tenderly held during those difficult periods, comforts me at a level that is beyond words.

Sweet Jim (1987)

Sweet Jim
    Your music moves me still
And opens my eyes
That's the real question
    Isn't it
Will I hang upon the lover's Cross for him
An act of love
    Beyond human dimensions
This is marriage the Sacrament
These are the movements of grace
I need only agree
    And I will be gently lifted up
    And tenderly held
By the One already on the lover's Cross
I believe in the Resurrection

* * *

These words passed through my thoughts one morning as I sat in a dark and quiet church. I wrote them down. I remember them.

(1987)

You absorb
I'll transform

*   *   *

With this poem, as with some others, I started by expressing my thoughts accurately. As it progressed I lost my focus. Again my reaction to this poem is one of indifference because I began to follow my own words and not the gentle flow of thoughts and feelings that had started me writing. When this happens I feel like I've switched levels - in a very real way - yet I don't wish to belittle my own words. I think they are fine, but I seem to switch into neutral when I read them. This thought returned at a later time and I wrote a poem which seemed to express what I had meant to say here. That poem is "SEEDS" (1988).

We are constantly listening to, weighing, rejecting, accepting and absorbing ideas. I have read and heard many inspiring and thought-provoking words over my lifetime. The wisdom of those writers and speakers has been incorporated into my thinking in a general way. A case-in-point is the "blue rose" of the poem. I read another poem years ago on that theme and the beautiful thought expressed has stayed with me. I feel very grateful to everyone who has inspired and challenged me to think and to grow over the years.

A Friend Said …(1987)

A friend said in passing
"The rose is in the seed"
and stunned me

Why had I never understood that before
        Not as common knowledge
        Not as a genetic truth
But as an incredible miracle

How profound
A continuous thread of life
        We are one with nature
        The same rules apply

If we do not want a rose
        We should not plant a seed
If planted
        But unwanted
We must remember
        Learn from it
Never plant another
But the planted rose lives
        Belongs
It has roots
        And purpose
It promises beauty and fragrance
It is a precious part of the whole
It Is

And what if we want a red rose
        And it comes up blue

The seeds are gifts
    We simply plant them
The Gardener plans the colour scheme

This blue rose
    A perfect complement to the other flowers
    Helps them to be more beautiful

The miracle is not in the colour
    It is in the rose
    And the rose is in the seed

* * *

Human Mirrors … (1987)

Human mirrors reflect goodness
    Failure
        Love
            Hatred

I turn to mine
    And feel crushed

Is it a distortion
    My faulty vision

Or painful truth

Oh No (1987)

Oh no
It looks like they're coming here
What could they want

Tell them I'm not home
No
Tell them we already give or belong or whatever

Really
People should be allowed the privacy of their own home

God knows
We pay enough taxes to live here

There's really no excuse for looking so unkempt
I know they're poor
But somebody must give clothes to people like that

Wouldn't you know
They're teenagers
Probably drifters

For heaven's sake
It looks like she's pregnant on top of everything else

That's the last straw
I'll answer the door myself

What's that you say
Your name is Mary

* * *

What Is (1987)

What is
Start with what is

I cried for what might have been
I dreamed of what should have been
I resented what would never be

All that time
    Energy
    Pain
Chasing shadows
Self-inflicted wounds
    Wasting precious moments
    Or years
    Draining my mind
            Exhausting my body
A devil wreaking havoc
    With my permission

Start with what is
Choose God
He lives in the now
    So do we

* * *

Although there may have been a time lapse between this experience and the poem, I do recall the incident which prompted me to think about pain.

The scandal with Jimmy and Tammy Faye Bakker had broken some time earlier. All of the jokes had circulated in papers, magazines and talk shows. We had enjoyed a few at our kitchen table - most of which probably came from me. Then one day I saw Tammy Faye on T.V. She was surrounded by reporters who were hollering and pushing microphones in front of her face. She had her head down, sobbing quietly. It wasn't funny any more. I was overwhelmed by feelings of compassion for her.

On Pain (1987)

Sometimes I hurt so much
        I feel raw
        Inside out
Even to look on me hurts

But life goes on
        And so do I
A very thin skin makes it possible

Looking normal
        Knowing my vulnerability
I feel alone
        But sense we are legion
        Invisible to each other

That is private pain
How does one bleed publicly
    And survive
For socially acceptable tragedies
    There are mourners in abundance
But what if the tragedy
    So deep
    With pain so sharp
Throws one into disgrace
Pariahs bleed alone
Their strength is a miracle

And what if the tragedy
Places one in public ridicule
People laughing at the pain
Photographing the agony

Could there be anything worse

Imagine experiencing every kind of
emotional pain
    Private
    Public
    Disgrace
    Ridicule

And then the physical agony
    Beatings
    Torture
    Murder

By choice
For love

* * *

I seemed to be basking in feelings that were extraordinary for me. I felt loved in an absolute, unconditional way. It was an always and forever sense that made me know how safe and lovable I was. It was like the sensation of an adored child having fun in the presence of the most loving, wise and wonderful parent. I felt relaxed and playful. This poem followed an attempt to do some small "good deed" which I don't recall.

Sometimes ... (1987)

Sometimes we play games
You know me too well
But I love it
I love You
      I say
      Here God
      This one's for You
      Alone
You say thank you
Can you really keep it for Me
Alone
      And I say
      Of course
      But it's so hard
When I do
God laughs
And says
Thank you
Congratulations
I love you

      * * *

To St. Anthony (1987)

My lifelong friend
    Thanks to you
A total stranger
    Thanks to me
I know nothing about your life
    Yet
    I suspect I owe you much
When God was
    At best
    Distant
    At worst
    Empty words and threats
    You were there for me
    Always

My request recited by rote
Your response consistent
Were you leading me from childhood games
To the discovery of my life

As your favours became more incredible
I began to believe in your power
And then slowly
In you
    And finally I said
If there really is a St. Anthony
Then maybe there really is a God

Thank you for being my compass
    And my bridge

The Lines Are Blurring (1987)

The lines are blurring
You spend more time with me
    In my reality
I spend more time with You
    In some other place

Sometimes
The real and unreal seem to switch places
I recognize You now
    Most of the time
    I hope
I know You to be true
    To be truth
You are often in my conscious life
    Opening doors
    Working with me
    Making the impossible possible

So many "real" events surrounding me
    Come from another place
They are symptoms
    Responses
Nothing is as it seems

I feel I'm straddling two worlds
It's miraculous
    But disorienting
I couldn't begin to direct my life from this place
I live by trusting You to lovingly care for me
    And I have never felt more secure

Today (1987)

Today
All my insecurities came rushing back
They didn't have far to come

I think of what I've written
And I feel disrespectful
  Arrogant
  Embarrassed
  Even foolish

As if I could really know You
Who do I think I am
And what would others say if they read my words

In a flash You're back on high somewhere
  Or worse
  Gone altogether
  And I'm alone
How did that happen

Then I see You looking at me
  Knowing me
  Loving me
  And gently asking
Who do you say I am?
And I know I know You
Intimately
  But in mystery

* * *

Images sometimes surface unexpectedly in my mind's eye and move me to express my thought and feeling in poetry. This was an image of a person with gentle waves passing through the entire body. The poem was written in response to the recurring but distant memory of that image. I realized that I had overlooked this experience at some time. Although I wrote this poem in the 1990's I inserted it into the 1980's because I guessed that it belonged there.

Locked Into Place

Locked into place
By circumstances
Without choices
Solutions
Or relief
I felt such desperation
You knew
Slowly
Miraculously
You moved through that space
In gentle waves of healing
You gave me room to breathe
To move
A sense of hope returned
You entered into my experience
And transformed it
On the spot

* * *

You Are ... (1987)

You are the antithesis of demands
   And threats
   And guilt
Your arms do not hold a whip
They are open wide in love
How did we do this to You
In Your name

They were blind
And crucified You
In ignorance

The crucifixion continues

You felt the pain horribly
Being human
How much more so
Being God
Are You still in pain

You Say … (1987)

You say we are one
That I live in You
Are You then asking me
    Inviting me
To be You
Not in word
In the flesh
To love the poor
To heal the sick
    With their invisible wounds
To speak of what I know
    In the Temple
To join You on the Cross

How could I want to do that
But I do
You really are in me

If You could do it
    I can
Is that what You're saying
I know the answer
    But the truth overwhelms

All my strength
    My only strength
    Is in You
Yet
    You live in me

Christ Spoke ... (1987)

Christ spoke of peace
    Love
    Forgiveness
    Eternal love
But we needed signs

So He said
    Pick up your cot
    Rise from the dead
    See
    Hear
    Walk

Christ broke bread
    And said
    This is My Body
    This is My Blood
But we needed signs

So He gave us His body
    He gave us His blood

Christ was the living bridge
    Between God and humanity
He still is
Eucharist lets us cross that bridge

*   *   *

It was a Saturday morning. I was aware that my mind had that sense of emptiness, or fullness, that I had come to recognize as "something-on-my-mind", which called for me to take some quiet time and allow the thought to unfold. But I didn't do that.

I remember parking in front of a bank. As I sat there I had an image of a very fine and beautiful white material blowing softly in a gentle breeze. It seemed as if something were open behind it - like a door. It was an experience of movement that seemed to be happening in that instant.

My first thought was, "I wonder if that's the 'diaphanous veil' that Teilhard de Chardin talked about." Although that was my first thought I have not been able to confirm that Teilhard de Chardin ever said those words.

The image returned several times that morning. This poem comes from that experience.

My Union With You (1987)

My union with You
      Something in the oneness
I know
      But I don't know what I know

Is Your life knowledge I already have
Is that why it feels so good to be at one with You
      Because I am at one with myself
Is that how I will know what to do
      Because I have somehow done it already

I cannot understand
Maybe
    I should not try
But I feel Your presence
    Your call to understand
    The movements of mystery
    That make no sense
    But perfect sense
I miss so much of what You say
    But I want to move as one with You
    To put on Your mind
Whenever You are ready
    Please make me ready

*   *   *

I Was Conscious (1987)

I was conscious
    And will be again
But the veil of original sin surrounds the now
It conceals my unconscious
    Separates me from my God
A journey inward thins out the veil
That inner harmony illuminates the now
    Resolves the conflicts

To sense the invitation is a grace
    To accept it is a choice

I Don't Know … (1987)

I don't know what You're asking of me
    And I feel panicky

I'm doing things I don't even know how to do
    As if I knew how to do them
    And I do

I feel like I'm listening to the radio
    But I'm the only one who can pick up the station

Things are moving so quickly
If I look down I start sinking
Like Peter
And I'm in so far over my head

You've brought me to a place
    That makes life without You impossible
I want to be here
    But I'm frightened
Is this feeling of foreboding
    A trick of my mind
    Or an insight from You

... Precious Vessel (1987)

I am a precious vessel
    Crafted lovingly by my Potter
    And by me
I can be a magnificent creation
    Or a plain but functional container
I alone will make that decision
    I have that power
    And freedom

I see plain
    I feel functional
How do I create magnificence
God has the creative genius to design
I have the power to fire the kiln
Where then is my will to succeed
    My energy to persevere

Sometimes I glow
    Or have done
It feels wonderful
    Energizing
    But risky
I can make bad choices
    And have
But not always
Focusing through Christ I can make beautiful choices
Good doesn't mean dead
God isn't gray
    But safe is

Now I See (1987)

Now I see
   More

You focus through me
    See through my eyes
    Listen through my ears
    Love with my love

You are my strength
   I am Yours

Eucharist feeds You
   In me
I distribute You to others
You are not the bridge
I am

Imagine (1987)

Imagine
If I could take every bit of me
        My senses
        My energy
        My mind
        My heart
        My soul
And apply them to this moment
I could drain it dry
        Extract everything it has to offer
        And move on

How strange
This is all I have anyway
Whether I live it through every fibre of my being
Or pass through it in a fog

The opportunities are boundless
 But passing

Please keep me in the now
        Alive
        Awake

Seeds (1988)

Seeds
    A world of seeds
    That's what we are

Everything that lives
    We are one
    Related
    A common heritage
    Equal
    Powerless
    Microscopic
    Yet
    Incredibly
    Miraculously
    Complete
    Balanced
In blessed harmony
Called into life
    To be
    To become
An invitation to grow
    Without limits
    Into the One who Is
Part of the code
Part of the roots
Part of the promise

Now It's Not Enough (1988)

Now it's not enough
To offer my problems
    My thanksgiving
    My weakness
My love is so much more than the parts

I offer You all of me
    All that I am
    In love
    For transformation

I am the bread
I am the wine
And how You welcome my offering
    Your love surrounds me
    Holds me close

You consecrate my body
You consecrate my blood
    And enter me
    Become me
    We are one

Finally I Understand (1988)

Finally I understand
    Not through wisdom
    Or maturity
But in spite of myself
    Through painful experience

Without You
    Truly
    I can do nothing

With You
    Anything
    Everything
    Is possible

I have lost control
    Gone to the brink
Or been brought
    In every part of my life
    With senseless repetition

Immersed in weakness
    Failure
    Shame
Blind to Your presence
You pick me up
    Carry me
    Lead me
    Love me
Until I'm back on track
    Stronger than ever

Free to make choices
Again

What a risk You take
Why
Do You love me that much

You give me the freedom to reject You again
And I do
But You have such faith in me

How could You know me so well
The me of the dark recesses
The deepest levels
The me I've never met

Either as Creator You know Your creation
Or that's where You are
Or both
There's no other way

I see Your miracles
And they are miracles
Repeated
Impossible
Acts of love

That's How We're Different (1988)

That's how we're different
    Isn't it
We share the same instincts
    To survive
    To nurture
    To attack
    To kill
But we have intelligence
    Judgement
    Free will
We understand community
    Propriety
    Laws
But You said more
    Lived more
    Died more
They said
    Attack
You said
    Love
They said
    Kill
You said
    Love
They said
    He
You said
    We
        Listen to Me
        Watch Me
        Follow Me

This Feeling … (1988)

This feeling is uncomfortable
        Sad
            Lonely
But familiar
So familiar

It feels like failure

I hear their messages
        Mixed
        Muffled
        Layered
But I can't get in step
I'm weary of trying
It doesn't seem to matter anymore

Teach Me … (1988)

Teach me to celebrate life
        Please

    To live Your gifts of
            Health
            Summer
            Love
            Laughter
            Wondrous chaos
Only in You is balance possible

Choices (1988)

Choices
    Made for me
    Not by me

Heartbreaking
    Humiliating
    Movements through blackness

Survival was holding on
    Head down
    Eyes closed
Alternatives eliminated
Aspirations destroyed

How could I know
    That was the price of admission
How can I ever thank You

How Can It Be (1988)

How can it be
Confused by fear
    We teach distance
        Deny equality
        Foster alienation
        Govern with institutional authority

Clearly
    Your invitation to love
    Calls for personal responsibility
    Promises Your wisdom
    Guarantees the power of love

Yet
    To act like You
    To talk like You
    To speak my truth

Sounds like heresy
    Even to me

I Know You're There (1988)

I know You're there
Just beyond my grasp
Reaching out
Always inviting me to take another step
So I struggle to touch
But I sense a shift
Another move
Deeper maybe
These spaces are strange
Beyond me in every way
Yet
I know I can follow
Any distance
To any level
Because You're leading me
And I will come
Because I love You
Where are we going

Wait (1988)

Wait
  Don't respond
  Not yet
Be still and open
My spirit within you
  Will lead you to Me
      In her
      In them
      In this situation
Then speak to that truth
  Connect with Me
  And you will find your answer
Touch the core
  Give Me life
I will do the rest

Is That Why … (1988)

Is that why people were drawn to You
    Not because You were Christ
    They didn't know that

But because we are drawn to truth and love
    We long to be a part of it
    Not understanding that we already are

When truth is spoken
    When love is lived
    You are calling to others

And they will hear You with their souls

To Kathy (1988)

Her name was freedom
   Her life was truth

With gentle hesitancy
   And stunning clarity
   She unmasked sham
   Rejected givens
   Spoke simple profound truth

My mind
   Or was it heart
   Or maybe soul
Watched
   Listened
           In astonishment
           In recognition
I knew this place
   This mind
It was mine
   Unshackled

A barrier was crossed forever

Like a joyful child
   In a field of wild flowers
My mind embraced freedom
   Danced
   Spun
   Did cartwheels
And loved me
   From out there

To return was unthinkable
  Undesirable
  Even to me

My playful child is maturing
  But wanders
  And searches
  Touching all things

Fearing nothing
  Beyond discipline
  I give her my blessing
No
More than that
I thank God
  Through tears of joy
  For my restless wanderer
  My seeker of truth
And for Kathy

Amazing
  The dream becomes reality

"Who Touched My Clothes?" (1988)

"Who touched My clothes?"
Who touched my soul
    Amid the crush of mega life

I felt it
I know it
I search in desperation
    To be touched again

I look into the eyes
    Listen to the tone
    Read the signals

My soul seeks union
    Responds deeply
    But knows only love
        Speaks only truth
    As souls do
        Crushing or life-giving truth

And the mind
    Ever alert
    Listens
    Understands
    Reacts

This complex creation
    Hums on the presence
Disintegrates on the absence
    Of love

I Wait (1988)

I wait
　In silence
　Having judged my worthiness
　For gifts of perfect love

I search their souls
　Seek out a purity
　A perfection
　Of intention
　　Depth
　　Desire

Failing that
　And this human love must fail
　　Does fail
I feel rejected
　And it hurts
　　And costs

Have I learned nothing from You
How could I be so blind

I am the one who rejects
　This beautiful human love
　　Imperfect
　　Faltering
　　Spontaneous

How can they ever forgive me
　Or know my love

An Invitation (1988)

Come
Relax with Me
Close your eyes
And face Me
Feel the warmth of My sun on your skin
And My gentle breeze through your hair
Listen
Birds taking flight
Sharing secrets
Take a deep breath
My fragrance soothes the soul
Lilacs with a hint of clover
Now open your eyes slowly
Look at what I've made for you
Past the lush banks of trees
And the rolling green hills
To the cool
Sparkling
Peace
Of My river
Bordered by layers of majestic hills
As far as the eye can see
And all under wisps of white
In the bluest of skies
In all the world
This moment is yours alone
And you almost passed it by

Christ Died For Love (1988)

Christ died for love
> His love for us
> His love for the Father
> His faithfulness to the Spirit of love

And passed on
> For all time
> Himself
> His Body and Blood
> Love and Truth personified

To us

He passed on love
> And the wisdom to know the truth of love

We receive
> Become
> Share
> Eucharist

We receive
> Become
> Share
> Love

We are love and truth personified

We Are Physical Beings (1988)

We are physical beings
   Gifted in our sexuality
Not a necessary evil
   A lower form of nature
But a central part of our being
   A force of beauty
    And joy
But we are missing Your message

Lies on all sides confuse me
I recognize the lies
   But I can't find the truth
Except in love
   As always

Is that it
It is not sex that we abuse
It is love

The Essence Of God ... (1988)

The essence of God is love
We are made in that image
 Because we come from that Source
That is the nature of our souls
 The essence of our being
To live otherwise
 Is to be in deep
   Basic
   Conflict
   With our centre
   With ourselves
Within us
 Is the only power on earth
 Which can transform every human life
   Solve every human problem
   Overcome every challenge of evil
We know the power
 We have seen it tested
   And proven
   Repeatedly
And we recognize it
But we don't understand it
 Won't trust it
 Can't control it
So we deny it

Something Is Different (1988)

Something is different
    Almost frightening
    But I'll get used to it
You've moved out of the background of my mind
    Off the Cross
    Out of the Tabernacle
Everything is so real
    So close
    That I need a new language
I can't ramble on
    To wandering images
You're right here with me
    And You're listening
I can't lose myself
    In memories of You
You're as alive in this moment as I am
I sense Your presence
    This new reality
But I can hardly believe it
We are walking together
You know that
    And now
    In Your beautiful gift to me
    So do I

Behind That Wall … (1988)

Behind that wall of many colours
    Is such beauty
    A precious treasure
Hearts
    And minds
        And souls
            Brimming over
                With intelligence
                  Humour
                  Ideas
                  Love
Needing only an invitation
They're right in front of us
    But we can't see them
    Or won't
God forgive our selfishness
    Our blindness

Or is it fear
So much fear
    Of the unknown
    Of the risk
    Of commitment
    Of our own mortality
It must be true then
    Fear
    Not hatred
    Is the opposite of love

Something Wonderful ... (1988)

Something wonderful is happening
      I can feel it
Deep wounds are healing
This miracle
      Unfolding in Your own time
      Has softened the senses
      Filtered them through the heart
Harsh truth
      Lies
Focusing though love
      Exposes deep and profound truth
      In all its wonder
      In all its fragility

Only You had that knowledge to share
      And You trust me with it

An awesome responsibility
      Given in love
      Carried in love
      By the two of us

I Gave You … (1988)

I gave You my problems
    You showed me solutions

I shared my haunting fears
    You filled me with loving security

I surrendered my will
    You gave me a freedom beyond my dreams

I am slowly exposing my soul
    You are exposing my traps and pitfalls

One by one
    I gave you parts of me
    Twisted
    Damaged
    Parts

But You didn't keep them
    You gave them all back
    Fixed

Today ... (1988)

Today I feel so angry
I'm tired of trying
It's always the same
Why should I absorb everything
Reflect on my reactions
Struggle with my feelings
Try to respond with love
Anger is appropriate
Or at least justified
It's so unfair
I deserve better treatment
I'm worth more than that
But I can't even feel this in peace
Whether or not I should
I'm afraid to let go
I don't know this anger
Where does it come from
Where is it going
What's hidden down there
Anger is frightening
But
To know myself
To be exposed
Is to disarm fear
O.K.
I'll try
Again

On Being "Woman" (1988)

The wisdom of our souls
        Hangs heavy round our necks

Always reacting
        Old tapes
        New shadows

The light disappears
        In the fog of misunderstanding

I reach out
        Helplessly
And touch a hand outstretched
I am not alone

Single Lives (1988)

Single lives
        Ordinary lives
        Centered in love
        Transform the world

A nation changes hands
A people find freedom
A planet takes notice

Again and again
        The Spirit emerges

Because they dared to trust
        The power of love

*   *   *

I was at a quiet weekday Mass when this happened. The first image I saw was the lower arm and hand of a man holding a goblet shaped like a chalice but fashioned of earthenware. The chalice was tipped away from him as if it were being offered to someone. He was standing on the left side of the image that was in my mind. What I saw was his right hand but from his position I assumed the goblet was being held with both hands. The sleeve of his garment was wide and hung loose from his wrist.

There was a time lapse without any image. Then, from the right, a woman held the goblet in her hands. I don't remember the sleeve of her clothing but I knew it was a woman. There could be no mistaking the difference in the hands. I assumed that she, too, was holding the goblet with both hands although I could see only her left one. The goblet had been accepted, raised and was tipped toward her.

These remain clear, strong and very moving images for me.

You Offer The Cup ... (1988)

You offer the cup to me
   With a closeness
   An intimacy
   I have never known
And I understand Your offer
   Your loving plea
Will I drink from Your cup
   With You

It feels binding
   Final
   A commitment
   So deep
   It is beyond words

Everything stops
   I sense the stillness
From somewhere within
   I understand this moment
And I drink from the cup

I have entered into something
Nothing will ever be the same again
   But I don't understand
What have I done
What does it mean

*   *   *

Our Journey ... (1988)

Our journey became visible
    Godliness became human
    To show humans our godliness

Every life begins in Bethlehem
    And ends in resurrection

Christ lives in the eternal now
    Always unfolding
    Never ending

As it was in the beginning
    Is now
    And ever shall be

All That Matters (1988)

All that matters
   In leading my life
   Is Your life

I focus on mine
   Remembering Yours
   And something happens

Miraculously
   The lines disappear
   Forwards
   Backwards

Our lives are being lived together
   In the present
   As two
   As one
Somehow
   The same life

How can it be
   But it is

You Held My Sentence … (1989)

You held my sentence in mid-air
   Unfinished
While I struggled with endings

I tried to say
   You came and . . .
      What
   You came and
   Left us Eucharist
No
   You came and
   Left us Your spirit
No
   You came and
   You stayed
My sentence ended

Your form has changed
   That's all
So many times
   So many ways
   You told us it would
You made the connections
   Over and over
Helping us
   Pleading with us
   To understand
   To trust your gift of wisdom
      That bridges mind and soul
      That gives us the eyes to see

You did what You said You would
You came and You stayed

Just as alive
Just as real
Your form has changed

That's all

How Can I Invite You … (1989)

How can I invite You in
You see this heart
    Soul
    Mind
    Body
And so do I
Full of gifts
    Wasted
    Ignored
    Abused
        Promises
            Unkept
        Resolves
            Unmet

    Dear Lord
        I am not worthy

Do You Need Us ... (1989)

Do you need us too
   Is this Your place of refuge
   As much as it is ours

Outside these walls
   Your pain must be endless
How can You stand it
   The denial
        Rejection
        Ridicule
        Isolation
   The darkness of Your world

In the light of our love
   You are safe
        Cherished
We join hands
   Moment to moment
   Around the world
   To protect You
   To love You
   To ease Your pain

We will not desert You

Gail Higgins

With Eyes Grown Used To Darkness (1989)

With eyes grown used to darkness
I stared into the empty mug
Cupped in my left hand
Right finger gripping the handle
And I thought about helplessness
    The outstretched hand

I watched in disbelief
    The movement of my fingers
Slowly
Gently
I felt the touch of my left hand
    Outstretched
It was so comforting

Whose touch was this
    Whose hand

Was this the answer to my question
I was not alone
I had all I needed
I had myself
With all the power
    The wisdom
    The love
To lead the way
    Through darkness
    Helplessness

God's gifts to me
I need only believe

I Dream ... (1989)

I dream of being Your faithful companion
    Your cherished friend
Predictable in my faithfulness
    Unswerving in my love
But reality shatters dreams

In the Garden
In Your moment of anguish
I would be there
I would promise You anything
And mean it

But I would be the first to fall asleep

With a broken heart
I would walk beside You
Without the crushing weight of the Cross
Without the agony of open wounds

I would mean to strengthen You
    With my presence
To comfort You
    With my love
But the pebbles in my sandal
    The flies around my dripping face
        Would win the moment

Pebbles and flies

While You died slowly
    In front of my very eyes

I Wonder (1989)

I wonder
  Have we misunderstood You

Were You really saying
  The wheat is My body
  The grapes are My blood

By recognizing that sacredness
  In all of creation
  We give thanks to the Creator
    For the created

We complete the circle
  As only humans can

  In that act of love
    You are there
        Connected
        One with us

The circle flows
  Unbroken

* * *

I woke up and sat on the side of the bed with great effort. At the time of this experience I was trying to stay off cigarettes - again - and I was struggling with weight gain - again. But, on this morning, I felt everything in the extreme. My body felt like dead weight and every part of me hurt. To turn my head, to bend my wrist, I ached with every movement. I was close to tears.

I remember saying, to myself or to God, that I would never make it to whatever inner level of growth was intended for me because my body was going to kill me first. I felt hopeless and very much at risk.

I stopped at Church on my way out to do errands. It was dark and empty. I walked up close to the Tabernacle but I didn't genuflect. I was sure I would be unable to stand again if I tried that.

I was confused and overwhelmed by my physical state but I had no idea how to turn things around. Every previous effort had been unsuccessful. I felt, quite literally, that my health was failing fast so I was desperate for guidance.

I asked God for answers or strength or wisdom or healing - something that would give me a chance at health again. Nothing happened.

After a time I left to do my grocery shopping. I remember parking the car but the car radio was still playing. I was no longer thinking about myself but my thoughts were in their usual jumble. Passing through them came the sentence:

"KNOW THAT YOU ARE HEALED"

I caught the words when they happened but I was confused by them. It said I had received what I was asking for - already. I couldn't imagine how that could be so - yet I knew, almost immediately, that it was true. At some level I was healed.

I do not doubt, for one instant, the words of that profound sentence but I continue to struggle with living that truth.

This poem was written some time later.

Go Home (1989)

"Go home
    Your son will live"
Know that you are healed
That's the same message
    Isn't it
Different only in form
    As You explained
God forgive my lack of faith
Why do I cling to my weakness
    My helplessness
Why do I refuse to acknowledge Your healing
Is it because of fear
    The fear of responsibility
        Of having to live up to Your gifts
The fear of risk
    I could lose my way again
    I could fail

I could look foolish
But not to You
What else matters
Besides
    You have dealt with my fear
    I know that

I give You each moment
    In love
    In thanksgiving
    In faith
Please show me how to live with the wholeness
    The integration
    The balance
    Of being healed

And in my weakness
    My moments of panic
    Please hold my hand

I do know Your power
    And I do believe

* * *

...Understand (1989)

I don't understand
So many unanswered questions
    New questions
But something seems different
    Turned around somehow
Is it really
    Here
    Now
Is the power of God
    The power of man

A human power accessible only through God

Somehow (1989)

Somehow
I know
We are Christ
We are the Spirit
Two out of three
I wonder
Are we also the Source
    The Creator
Are we the Trinity
Is that how we are one with You
    We are You

If I am wrong
    Please show me
If I am right
    What does that mean

Like A Soft Wave … (1989)

Like a soft wave across my mind
I wondered
Will I disown You too
Surely
    That could never happen
Anything is possible
    But I'm on guard
    I'll see it coming

I don't declare my love for You publicly
    In so many words
With some shame
    And sense of cowardice
    I tell myself
    That's not my style
I'll live my love
    Or I'll try
In my private world
    My deeply personal world
    I love You
    I choose You
There
At least
I would never disown You

How soon the test
How total my failure

In my private world
My deeply personal world
I sensed Your presence

I saw my choices
And I disowned You
Even there
Without any threat to my person
Without a gathering storm of accusations
I failed You
Totally

I feel sick
Is there anything I am not capable of

Only The Shepherd (1989)

Only the shepherd
Is recognized by the sheep
His voice unique among sounds
Known at some instinctive level
Trusted
Followed

Only the shepherd
Faithfully watches over his flock
Senses the dangers
Rescues the helpless
Loves each sheep individually
    Totally
    Equally

Only the shepherd
Can see the whole pasture
Knows when to set the sheep free
And when to call them home

... The Garden (1989)

Are we still in the garden
Are You the garden
To understand our place
Is to understand Your presence everywhere
Looking through Your eyes
Lets us see the garden as it really is
Lush
Abundant

Is that our godliness
Coming from that place
Gives us Your miraculous touch
Human wounds heal
Animals thrive
Land blossoms

Without You
We see the garden as hostile
Threatening
A jungle

Is that the possibility of life
To create heaven
Or hell

Is This The Feast ... (1989)

Is this the feast You have prepared for us
            Magnificent in its beauty
            And abundance

Food
Drink
Places
For everyone

Each person special
            Invited by the Host

The guests distribute the provisions
            Seat themselves at the table

And then wait
            We all wait
            For the Bridegroom

I Don't Understand (1989)

I don't understand
One Creator
One Source
One faithful Jewish life
An explanation
Not a denial
Of our spiritual roots

Are we all Jewish

One truth of love
The same truth
The same wisdom
For every age
In every life

To move closer to You
In division
Amid human barriers
Is impossible for me
You are unity
    Oneness
Your Spirit dissolves boundaries
Why can't we do the same

Life Is God (1989)

Life is God
Surrounding us
  In trees
    Air
      People
We live in Him
  Within Him
He lives in us
  Within everything that exists
Truly
The Alpha
  And Omega
The Shepherd
  And the lamb
The Creator
  And the created
God
  And man

The eternal paradox

Trees (1989)

Sometimes
Surrounded by your towering strength
And touched by your gentle invitation
I enter your world
And feel like crying in gratitude

How could I ever survive without you
Without my favourite touchstone
My wise and generous friend

You talk to me about seasons
Warn me of approaching storms
Cool my body
And delight my soul
With your soft rustling breezes

You work such wonders with wind
Such magic with moonlight
Sunlight

Lovingly
I watch you grow
From struggling infancy
Through awkward youth
And proud young adulthood
To the quiet strength of middle age

Speechless
I marvel at the awesome glory
Of your farewell performance

But
Strangely
In your November bleakness
I need you most
You remind me of our common truth
Your mantle of simplicity
 Stillness
So essential for life
Conceals your quiet growth
Your return to your roots for strength

You change my winter from despair to hope
We both wait in faith
For the promise that is spring

* * *

During the Consecration of the bread and wine, I had this experience of the flowing sense of movement from the altar through the Crucifix and up to God. The angle of Christ on the Cross in this image reminds me of the suspended figure of Christ in Salvador Dali's painting "Santiago El Grande" but my experience seemed larger and closer. It was a beautiful feeling of the continuous upward flow from us through Jesus to God.

Your Perfect Creation (1990)

Your perfect creation
    Made a perfect offering
    The ultimate gift of love
    To You
    To us
The gift for all time
In our now
    We take Your created gifts
    And step into that forever moment
    We give thanks
    And unite with You
    In an upward stream of light and love
Our gifts
    Through our crucified Jesus
    To You
Our gifts
    Become the Body and Blood of Christ
    A living perfect sacrifice of love
In this union
We are one
    Amen

*   *   *

... Blackness Of Despair (1990)

In the blackness of despair
> When our pain is unbearable
> Our temptations overwhelming

You are there
You say
> Trust Me
> The wall is not solid
> No matter how it looks to you
> Hold My hand
>> Now
>> Take one more step
> And walk through the wall

The answers are on the other side
In that one step
> Everything becomes possible

* * *

This feeling happened one quiet morning on my way up to Communion. I was completely lost in my own thoughts. I remember feeling distracted and worried about something. As I rounded the corner of the side aisle heading toward the priest at the centre aisle, I looked up at him distributing Eucharist. In that instant I felt a wave of recognition and relief and great comfort wash over me. I had recognized the presence of my trusted friend. It's hard to explain but it was something that I felt and knew more than something I saw.

Oh (1990)

Oh
There You are
Thank God
My Friend
My Confidant
Waiting for me
You are really there
And You're waiting
I could cry in gratitude
I'll be all right
I always am
Once we're together
In conversation
Or silence
Please wait
I need You
I love You
I'm coming

* * *

Pain (1990)

Pain
The great manipulator
Ignored
Denied
Dismissed
It lives
The terrorist within
Holding us hostage
Keeping us vulnerable
Dictating our responses
Confronted
Understood
Accepted
It dies
We grieve
We let go

A miracle of healing
A promise kept

Our choice
Pain
Buried dead
Or
Buried alive

* * *

This poem came from a combination of thoughts. I had been reading about a recent advance in the field of radiology. The newspaper article mentioned the ability of this technology to pick up "hot spots" in the human body.

I had also been thinking about those who help the needy day in and day out. In this instance I had been thinking less about an economic distinction than about the deep emotional wounds borne by so many. Some action by the Sisters of Charity in our area had started me thinking about all the incredible people of this world who heal the wounded. Having read about a few of them I realize that they do not see themselves as angels or saints or martyrs, nor do they appreciate being seen that way. I know they are regular human beings who are as good and as bad, as weak and as strong as the rest of us. To make them exceptional is to absolve ourselves of responsibility. I understand that, but I remain in awe of their quiet commitment to live love and to do it for the long haul.

How Miraculous (1990)

How miraculous
Human x-rays
   Of a sort
Scanning the world
   The crowd
   The room
   The heart

Hot spots
Of pain
Of agonizing need
   Recognized
   Treated
   Healed

Incredible
Hearts
Souls
Pain
   Not invisible
   Seen through the eyes of God
   Seen through the eyes of love

In a TIME magazine article entitled "THE END" by Michael D. Lemonick (16) about the cover story "HOW THE UNIVERSE WILL END" I read the words, "So some scientists began looking for subtle *hot spots*." (My italics.) I have no idea if there is a connection but the use of the exact same words or phrase always stops me in my tracks. I hope I will have a chance to think about that more deeply someday soon.

*   *   *

Listen … (1990)

Listen to yourselves
Why are you so vague
Not daring to question
Giving blind faith to interpreters
Please
Care enough
To search
Challenge
Dissect
Question
To touch My truth
Gifts
From Me
Because
I want you to know Me

Alone (1991)

Alone
Dark
Tangled
I kneel in silence
Waiting for You
In one wondrous instant
I recognize Your presence
In the light of possibilities
Open
Boundless
Waiting for me
An invitation
To enter into

* * *

I had a moment of awareness or understanding that I cannot explain very well. This type of experience happened more than once.

I was directing my thoughts to God but what came into my mind was something about myself. They happened at the same time. It reminded me of some kind of reflection or mirror that was showing me a truth about myself. At least, the effect felt the same.

Is That It (1991)

Is that it
Is that who I meet in Eucharist
Myself
Reflected back to me through You
In seeing You
I see myself
As You see me
Real
True
Eternal
I am

* * *

Please (1991)

Please
God
Must I drink from this cup
Slowly
The fog lifts
I remember
Not my cup
Our cup
We drink together
   Please
   No
   Must I hang on this cross
   Again
   Slowly
   I remember
   The Crucifix
   The lover's cross
   You are there first
   Waiting to hold me
   You share my pain
   We are crucified together
I saw Your presence
I do remember
I do believe
My God
My Comforter
My Friend
We cry together
We heal together
I am not alone

Now (1991)

Now
We are innocent
We are redeemed
We are free

The intervention of now
Releases us from our past
Opens all doors

Now is new
Now is alive
Now is real
Now is eternal
Now is God

What Do You Need (1991)

What do you need
    Is that love's message
Slavery
    Servitude
    Concepts out of time
Strength
    Known
Power
    Understood

"Love asks
    What do you need me to be for you" (17)

*   *   *

I recall this experience as an image in three parts but they flowed as one: the back of a body facing the Light of God, the body turned around in front of the Light, and edges of the body disappearing as it filled with Light.

What I felt was so wonderful that I have returned to the image many times for comfort and security. It felt like I was "home" - surrounded by the strength and the presence and the love of God. We were looking at my life together. I recall feeling very relaxed with God - almost as if He had His arms around me or resting on my shoulders but the image was, as always, Light.

In Absolute Trust (1991)

In absolute trust
    And love
Knowing my helplessness
    And Your presence
I come to You
From that place
    I turn round
    And face my life
We look on it together
Your Light
    Fills me
    Shines through me
    Becomes me
Margins disappear

I am Light
Again
I understand my body
   As a shell
   Container of the Light
Neither good nor bad
It brings me to You
   But confines nothing
      Dictates nothing
Softly
   It fades
      Unnecessary
      Irrelevant

Is that all death is
Is that what life is
To bring Light to the world
To be Light in the world

*   *   *

This experience of absorption has stayed with me over the years as a memory and as an ongoing possibility. I can almost see it in my mind.

The first time it happened I was with two people whose conversation was filling me with deep despair and hopelessness.

I remember asking God if He could help me to do more than cope. I wondered if it would be possible to move right through acceptance and come out the other side feeling positive about this situation.

Before that conversation ended, I was sitting in the same place with the same people but with a totally new mindset. It was so amazing to me that I had to recognize it for the incredible gift and grace that it was.

Confronted … (1991)

Confronted by a problem
    Often overwhelmed by its magnitude
We respond
With denial
Or martyrdom
Flailing helplessness
Or burdening of others
But
Another possibility exists
A deliberate choice
Of absorption
A hand in hand movement with God
To absorb the problem
    Is to face it
    And walk through it
    Beyond its existence

This transfer of power
    To our waiting
        Healing
        Creator
Allows for transformation
    Of our problem
    Of our vision
    Of ourselves

*   *   *

This poem is about the devastating grief felt by survivors after the death of a loved one. The image returned several times before I wrote this. It showed the upper body of a person whose head was bent forward, chin close to the chest. The flames were moving and surrounding this grieving person continuously.

Flames (1991)

Flames
White hot flames
Searing the soul
A consuming fire
Mercilessly
Consuming nothing
Head bowed
Anguish unbearable
Standing
Motionless
Powerless
Burning in pain
Choices eliminated
Save one
Life
Or death

* * *

Who Will Ask Me (1991)

Who will ask me
What do you need
Please
Where are You
I can't feel Your presence
I can't feel anyone's presence

Forgiveness (1991)

Forgiveness
I wonder
Did we misunderstand You
Your call to freedom
Your focus of wholeness
When You said
"Whose sins you shall forgive
They are forgiven"
Did You mean
They are forgiven
Within us
Whose sins we shall retain
They are retained

By us

This Darkness (1991)

This darkness
This poison blackness
Overtakes me
Everything I think
Do
Say
Everyone I touch
I wanted to be Your light
A source of peace
Of love
In my small world
What happened
What buttons got pushed
Am I stuck in martyrdom
Or worse
I forget how to absorb
I don't know how to get out of this ugliness
Yet
Nothing holds me
Except my anger
My desire to lash out
To poison the silence
Seems the better option
Is that it
Do I really desire to stay in this place
Please
Help me to let go
Walk me through this quiet rage
Above it
Beyond it
Help me to choose again

Sitting Alone (1992)

Sitting alone
In the dark
On a warm summer night
I delighted in the beauty around me
My favourite time
My favourite place
As I looked up at the soft rustling leaves
I caught a glimpse of something startling
Somehow
The sparkling blackness
As I had never seen it before
In the stillness
The foreverness of the universe
I felt the depth of eternity
Surrounding us
Completely
I felt both sad and frightened
My beloved moving world
Just a blip
From seed to ash

* * *

I made a deliberate choice not to do something I planned to do. I chose to stop, to sit down and to listen to someone who was in great emotional pain. In a rare moment of focus I seemed able to give him my full attention.

Something happened. It seemed to be a shift in dimensions. He became my total focus, fully alive before me; while everything else seemed still and distant. That's hard to explain because all of the objects around us were inanimate but they seemed to be on some other level, almost frozen in time. We two seemed to have a total connection.

When this experience ended I remember my thoughts as I sat there. I recognized that it had happened and I began thinking about miracles. I wondered if Jesus operated in that miraculous space. When He was working a miracle did He suspend time somehow and work in a different dimension of reality?

I Had A Moment (1992)

I had a moment
One awesome moment
Of total presence
Of perfect focus
A place within
Clearly
Someone else
Within my mind
My soul
Within
Or maybe

At one with
In this graced place
I knew the pain
I understood each word
A holy instant
Somehow
I think
A place of miracles

*   *   *

Christ (1992)

Christ
My entry point
Through the walls of this world
The walls of my mind
To the reality of truth and love
How many openings surround us
But we do not recognize them
Or trust them
Looking back
One sees
The wall was never there
Another illusion
In this world of illusions

*   *   *

In this image there was a winding road going up a hill or mountain. The road was passing on the right side of the mountain. Ahead it continued upward and curved to the left and out of sight. The slope rose rather steeply to the left of the road but had a more gentle grade on the other side. The grass was lush, the road was clear and clean and everything was bathed in sunshine. Someone was sleeping on the grass to the right of the road.

My feeling was one of absolute safety and security, as if someone were watching over me and the entire area. It was a beautiful spot to sleep peacefully. It felt like an invitation to rest on my journey for as long as I chose - with God's blessing and protection.

... So Very Tired (1992)

I'm so very tired
I need to rest here
Curled up on the roadside
I'm on the right road
I know that
I will move forward
I know that too
But not now
I must sleep
In the safety of Your presence
In the warmth of Your love
Please
Let me sleep away
The burden of complexity
The weariness of self-pity
The sadness of isolation
The misery of failure
You will gently
Heal my wounds
Transform my burdens
Awaken me refreshed
Thank You

* * *

Here is another experience of directing my thoughts to God but having them reflect back on me. I was attending a small, intimate Mass. The celebrant was a priest for whom I have great respect.

He was talking about forgiveness. This is a subject that usually causes my thoughts to become a little agitated. I have long wondered whether our focus on guilt, collective and individual, and our sense of sinfulness and unworthiness are really misguided and destructive. All of the words we use around this subject make me restless - sin, bad, evil, punishment, Hell, penance, judgement, guilt.

Usually I won't "operate" in that area. My thoughts are elsewhere - consciously or unconsciously - but because this particular priest was speaking about forgiveness I opened up to his words.

What I expected was not what I found. Forgiveness was a beautiful, loving area that, for me, in that instant, was filled with light. It had nothing to do with those words I mentioned. It had to do with love. It was very liberating to discover something else that existed - already. I felt it wasn't my truth but *the* truth.

I think I had seen forgiveness as separate from love, something we needed to ask for or hope for. Now I wonder if forgiveness is a gift that love gives by its very nature.

... Oneness Of Minds (1992)

Something in the oneness of minds
Of purpose
I don't understand
But I see it in forgiveness
I seek it
And find Your truth
Reflected back to me
Somehow
In that moment
We know the same thing
We share the same thought
I discover what is
What always was
And I am transformed
I know my forgiveness
I know everyone's forgiveness

Is that how love is
When I truly seek it
I will recognize it
Everywhere
A mutual recognition
A shared knowledge
Is it in that holy space
That we are transformed
That miracles happen
Do we have the power
            to change what we see
By changing how we see it

*   *   *

On this particular day there was some mention made of alms in the words of the Mass. I began to think that alms may be about money but they are also about much more than money.

It seems to me that the world is full of saints who give quiet gifts of love every day of their lives. I know this is so because I've known such people in my life so I believe they are everywhere.

I'm not talking about people who articulate their faith or even recognize, consciously, a greater power in their lives - although they may do both. I'm referring to their goodness, their courage, their acts of love which transcend their own struggle and pain.

Circumstances of serious illness, poverty and areas of war come immediately to mind but so does the daily struggle with loneliness, addiction, loss and failure.

Sometimes I wonder, seriously, if we are all saints because life is hard yet we endure and, on occasion, we are able to reach out to others in selfless acts of love. Other times we may have just enough faith in life that we allow ourselves to survive for one more day.

I should add, if I am to be honest, that I have many problems with "official" sainthood - not with the people but with the process. I wonder about the conferring of an elevated status on some over others. If only one group assumes the power to name saints, why do they choose them all from the same faith - out of billions of people?

Alms Giving (1992)

Alms giving
So many loving gifts of self
Given quietly
Privately
By the countless saints of this world
Their joyful presence
Their acts of love
Receive no public acclaim
How can we begin to know
The depth of love
Of gratitude
In the One who sees everything
The One who receives each precious alm

                              *   *   *

Untouched (1992)

Untouched
By the laws of nature
The biological decline of time
Our spirit grows
Deepens
The gifts are boundless
There for the asking
Wisdom
Understanding
Love
Spiritual blossoms
Flower with age
A natural upward movement into oneness

I Wonder (1992)

I wonder
Is that why we grow old
Instead of dropping off in strength
Is it another sign from You
A gift
A gentle constant reminder
That life is short
Temporary
All around us
Within us
Systems falter
Wind down
Each one another invitation
To search beyond the body for meaning
To understand our purpose here
You promised answers
We need only ask the questions
And then listen
In stillness

In Pain …(1992)

In pain and utter helplessness
Disasters looming
I gave You the day
And begged for miracles
Step by step
You moved us forward
Hours passed
Another hurdle
Another miracle
You gave us guidance
Strength
Consolation
Through You
With You
We survived
No
More than that
Into this chaos of emotion
Came a sense of peace
Your light
Into the darkness
Dear God
Thank You

Why Is It ... (1993)

Why is it so hard
To live in the present
This constant gift of intervention
This chance to choose again
This place where life is happening
To let go of plans
Preconceived notions
To live awake
Wide open to possibilities
Is to be fully alive
We're so busy
Planning the future
Based on the past
Recreating history

We Meet (1993)

We meet
In the beauty
Of this secret garden
Only You know the way
With the ease of deepest friendship
In absolute trust and love
We share this moment
Relaxing together
Breathing the same air
I rest in You
The silence so peaceful
If You speak
I will hear

I Wonder (1993)

I wonder
Is it natural human weakness
Or something else
Deep and original
That keeps us unfocused
Slipping out of the present
Away from You
Through daydreams
Memories
Worries
Plans
        When my mind is full
        Busy with distractions
        I cannot connect with You
        Where You are
        The only place that You are
        Here
        Now
        In this moment
        Waiting for me
If I will not clear a quiet place for You
I cannot understand You
Or the possibilities of this moment
To stay in the present with You
Empty and open
Is a choice I must make
        Union is possible
        So real
        Almost frightening
        I know
        But I don't understand

I Don't Understand (1993)

I don't understand
Another paradox
I have a need
A deep and enduring need
To be by water
I am nourished by the stillness
The vastness
The sounds and smells of the sea
I love the drama of crashing waves
But
As the tide rolls back
Toward me
A wave of something
Rolls across my mind
And
Always
When high tide
Pounds on breakwaters
This forever force
Frightens me
Deeply
At some level
Why do I fear
My great love
Is it my powerlessness
There is no reasoning with the sea
Or do I stand in opposition
Learn from the seagulls
I say
Accept the power
Trust it

Follow the shifting shoreline
Discover its perfect nourishment
Ride the waves
Of
With
The great Provider
Sustainer of life

What I Know Is (1993)

What I know is
I don't know anything
How can I react
I don't understand
What is really happening
I try to move gently
Certain always of love
I wait for understanding
Certain always of answers

Today (1993)

Today
I feel sick inside
How can I be
Where I think I am
In this relationship
What are You going to ask of me
Where is everyone else

To Recognize Truth (1993)

To recognize truth
Is a graced moment
A gift
To recognize something known
To remember what we know
In this living moment
Is to remember God
Now
To know Him
Now
An awesome experience
A reality so true
So clear
That all else pales
Somehow
A place removed
A timeless place of oneness
"Remember Me"
Remember that you know Me
A request so dear
A call so gentle
"Remember Me"
"Do this in remembrance of Me"

To Recognize Truth - Revisited (1999)

I entered into the stillness
And knew the tenderness
Of Your presence
So deep
Almost
An aching call of
Remember Me
Remember that you know Me
A request so dear
A call so gentle
A reality so clear
That all else pales
A place removed
A timeless place of oneness

I Asked … (1993)

I asked for Your help
In this difficult relationship
Having reached a point
Where trying was no longer enough
Beyond that
I knew I need do nothing
Standing together before You
One quiet Sunday morning
Something miraculous happened
I recognized it instantly
Like a splash
Somehow
Maybe a flash of light
Every obstacle between us
Disappeared
As if it had never existed
Everything changed
Without a word being spoken
In place of tension
Came trust
Relaxation
Flowing conversation
Laughter
A new starting place
Clearly
A gift from You
How faithful and present You are
I gave You a problem
In faith
You gave me a solution
In love

I Believe … (1993)

I believe I understand
Get behind me Satan
I feel that so deeply sometimes
I want to brush him away
With a movement of my arms
It's so real
This feeling
I want to stay open
I seek only God's wisdom
His truth
I want to know
I need to know
But a jumble of thoughts interferes
Foggy perceptions
Of power
Fear
Acceptance
No
I reject that
Get behind me Satan
I am clearing a path
I choose to wait
In stillness
For guidance
I choose love

* * *

Because of my experiences I was becoming aware of what I refer to here as "glimpses of heaven." When I tried to write about that thought I couldn't find any words that would equal those I read in *A Course in Miracles.* I don't know now whether these are an exact quotation or whether I paraphrased them. The lines begin with "In that instant" and end with "and with ourselves."

The Question ... (1993)

The question is not
Is there life after death
Is there life after life
There is life
Period
Our one same continuous life
It always was
It always will be
We catch glimpses of it
"In that instant
When we are transported beyond ourselves
Unaware of our bodies
Boundaries disappear
We sense a peace with all creation
And with ourselves"
Glimpses of Heaven
Here
Now
If glimpses are possible
So is more

* * *

Another First (1993)

Another first
Recognized instantly
But I wonder
I know the givens of my life
I trust Your thoughts more than mine
I deliberately defer to Your wisdom
I try to understand Your will
Because I find my answers there
Always the right answers
In this request for help
I was weighing the possibilities
The need
My ability
Or lack of
When I found myself responding
An instant of shock
Of catching up to my words
I was committing
Out loud
Before deciding to speak
Yet
Clearly
It was the right decision
A strange and new experience
Slightly alarming
Is this how it will be sometimes
Or was it some mental slip
Maybe something
Maybe nothing

Beyond Pleasantries (1994)

Beyond pleasantries
I falter
I am someplace
That doesn't fit
I know that
Very soon
Everyone does
What do I sense
Regret
Maybe pity
Confusion
Boredom
Some gap is widening
Laughter isn't joy
Fun isn't peace
Should they be
Have I lost something
Or found a treasure beyond words
I accept this instability
Filled with security
This isolation
Without loneliness
This space where we meet

... My Answer (1994)

Is that my answer
Is that how I see You in others
By understanding
That everything I know of You
In my life
Is true in every life
No specialness
No half-truths
Recognized or ignored
What is
IS

I Believe (1994)

I believe
    That life is not a test
    That love transforms
    That people are equal
    That our limitations are self-imposed
    That everything is sacred
    That power is meaningless
    That questions have answers
    That my mind is free
    That my spirit is free
    That God is real

Eucharist (1994)

Eucharist
Christ
Love
A miraculous space
Beyond human bounds
Moments lived through this space
Create
Miraculous
Boundless
Results

What We Seek ... (1994)

What we seek in our human relationships
Unconditional love
Acceptance
Trust
Faithfulness
Presence
Strength
Understanding
Happiness
Is what You offer
I wonder
Do these universal human needs
Come from the soul

... Time (1994)

Something about time
And dimensions
Again and again
I discover through You
That what I seek
I have already
That what I wait for
Already exists
If I connect
These moments of truth
Will I discover
That everything already is
Real
Unchanging
Timeless
So must we be
Or we couldn't connect
So what is life
Why is life
If we are not of time
Why do we live in time
Do we live in time
Or is it some kind of illusion
To be passed through
In a lifetime
Or an instant
Illusions disappear
Once recognized
Then what

* * *

I was at Sunday Mass when the experience captured in the following poem occurred. I had been consciously trying to think my way through what I had learned about Eucharist. I knew there was some "space" where God existed and where I had been. I thought I might be able to bring a concern of mine to this space and find answers for myself or healing for someone else. Sometimes I have a rather strong sense that I know or should know more than I do - more than I remember or know how to use. It seems to be very close but I can't grasp it. On this occasion, after Communion, I returned to my pew and rested my head on my hands briefly. When I looked up I saw an amazing sight. In front of me were about twelve pews filled with people and, in front of them, the altar, the priest and the altar servers. (This entire scene was within a space slightly larger than a semi-circle which had a pale but distinctive neutral colour.) I felt that I knew it was a circle although only the top half of it was visible to me. Once again I was amazed to discover that the space I was trying to find was where I was - already.

Once Again (1994)

Once again
You rearrange my thoughts
And lead me forward
Gently

I tried to move myself
My mind
Into Your miraculous space
To focus on a problem of my choice
At a time of my choice
What I found
Again
Is that what I sought
I had already
In a way almost beyond comprehension
The space I sought to focus through
Enveloped all that is
It is where I live
It is my home
This space does not exist outside of me
I exist within this space

*   *   *

* * *

In the mid 1980's I saw a video called "The Global Brain" by Peter Russell (18). (In the U.K. it is called "The Awakening Earth".)

The video had a profound effect on me, in a mind-expanding kind of way. I was deeply thrilled and filled with wonder at the possibilities which flowed from the ideas it contained. (I've seen the video a number of times since, always with the same effect.)

Russell's gentle, searching words invite the viewer "to think and to be" in a new way - to reflect on human, biological, global and planetary questions, on the evolution of consciousness. He speaks of those people around the world who are developing "leaky margins." These "leaky margins" occur when what is within them becomes more "one" with what surrounds them. When I was preparing this book that comment stirred me to revisit my poem - "In Absolute Trust" (1991) - which contains an image where the margins of my body began to disappear as light flowed through them.

Then during our summer vacation in 1990 my son encouraged me to read *A Brief History of Time* by Stephen Hawking (19). Although I didn't really understand or retain it, I enjoyed it. On a number of occasions Dr. Hawking's words connected to my thoughts in unexpected ways but I repeatedly dismissed that connection as illogical.

One such experience, however, made me rethink my position. I was already deep in thought about Hawking's statement, "We now know that every particle has an antiparticle, with which it can annihilate." I was thinking about the possibilities that exist with every action in our lives. Then I read, "The force-carrying particles exchanged between matter particles are said to be virtual particles because, unlike "real" particles, they cannot be directly detected by a particle detector. We know they exist, however, because they do have a measurable effect: they give rise to forces between matter particles." That made me think, "Isn't that interesting! We could say the same thing about love." I couldn't move from this thought. I became aware of the pressing intensity of the instant, maybe slightly fearful because it was a new form of experience, yet conscious of the fact that I should not dismiss what was happening.

I assumed I should pay more attention to my thoughts so I began to wonder if there were some connection between what I knew of human experience and Hawking's view of the universe's experience. At one point in *A Brief History Of Time*, he mentions that a two dimensional creation would be cut in half if something passed through its body. Again I was particularly struck by those words, as I remembered my experience (which I described in Chapter 10) of seeing my body split in half and filled with light.

At the same time as I was reading *A Brief History Of Time* I began looking through a LIFE magazine bought because I was amazed by the cover photo of a fetus within the uterus. The statement accompanying this photo said "The First Pictures Ever Of HOW LIFE BEGINS." The photographs taken by Lennart Nilsson (20) were stunning, truly breath-taking. The article was called "The First Days Of Creation." At one point Nilsson said, "These nuclei, drawn inexorably toward each other..." I thought, "I just read those exact words, I'm sure, about the actions of the universe." But I couldn't find them again in Dr. Hawking's book. I began to wonder if our internal universe and our external universe and what I had come to understand spiritually flow together. As so often happens, I couldn't begin to know or understand if or how Peter Russell's words about our expanding consciousness, Dr. Hawking's words about the birth of the universe and its ongoing expansion and Lennart Nilsson's "chronicle of human development from its first second" were connected, but the blending continued in my mind from time to time.

Because I try to follow through on my thoughts I decided to write Dr. Hawking a letter. I told him he had "added greatly to the richness of my confusion". Receipt of my letter of August 3rd 1990 was acknowledged with thanks on September 27th, 1990. It was sent from this address:

S.W. Hawking, CH CBE FRS,
Lucasion Professor of Mathematics
Department of Applied Mathematics and Theoretical Physics
University of Cambridge

It stated, " He hopes that you will appreciate that he is unable to write you personally."

I've always wished I could rewrite that letter because I didn't express my thoughts clearly - not even my central question. I wanted to ask him if he thought it possible that all acts of creation are the same - are unfolding in the same way - differing only in form. And if that is so could we then understand one form of creation better by examining and understanding another?

Again (1994)

Again
I am struck
By the sameness of things
The same patterns
The same rules
I wonder

Hawking says
Our universe is expanding
Rapidly
Russell says
Our consciousness is expanding
Rapidly
We know
You are extending through us
Rapidly
Is that a coincidence
They feel the same
Somehow

* * *

... Our Sinfulness (1994)

It's not that we don't know our sinfulness
It's that we don't know our forgiveness
Is that our purpose in life
To understand our own forgiveness
And then to allow that understanding
To be passed on through us
That forgiveness already is
For everyone
A reality
Waiting to be recognized
Bringing freedom
Deep peace
Quiet certainty
Salvation
It already is

Like The Petals ... (1994)

Like the petals of a flower
Slowly unfolding
In the warmth of the sun
I feel myself beginning to relax
To trust
To let go
I feel safe
To take risks
To love deeply
To be open

... The Final Illusion (1994)

Is that the final illusion
The separate self
That I thought I was
I am not
Today
I can't remember
The joy of that Oneness
Everything is upside down
It is threatening
It is loss
Or takeover
To lose myself
To disappear into Oneness
How can I want that
I like what I know
And feel
And want
What about my freedom
To choose
To err
To be good
To be bad
Can it be true
We're not side by side
We're the same
Is that it
Somehow
I never was

The Message ... (1994)

The message repeats
The thread connects
You are asking us
To unlock the door
When we meet someone
Locked in his own prison
That is our need
That is our gift
To open the door

Somehow
It must be opened for us
Before we can understand
That it was never there
Always the paradox
Or maybe the illusion
We need to give
And receive
Forgiveness
Before we can understand
That our sins were never there

To unlock the door
To offer forgiveness
Heals wounds
Which dominate our lives
But which were never there
A space for miracles

Is it easier to say
Your sins are forgiven
Or
You are healed

Living Self-Consciously (1994)

Living self-consciously
Is to keep myself in focus
To be an observer
I block my view
I become the obstacle
In my own path
The filter
Through which
Everything must pass
Arriving judged
Labelled
Living un-self-consciously
Is to let go
To become real
Open
Fully alive in the moment
With an unobstructed view

I could get out of my way
I could get out of Your way
And let You connect directly
Through me

I Can't Take It ... (1994)

I can't take it anymore
I can't manage a complicated life
I am overwhelmed
Clearly out of my depth
I'm dropping back
I give You the lead
I need to rest
And breathe
And regroup
Somehow
I know I can do this
That You will be there for me
And You are
I give up control
Completely
And life just hums along
It works
How incredible
It really works

* * *

This was a visual image of someone about to smash
something on the ground. With one leg forward and bent the
person held a round object overhead with both hands.

God (1994)

God
I hate this place I'm in
I resent everybody
I feel sorry for myself
I want to lash out
At somebody
Or something
Maybe myself
I am my own victim
Ignoring my own needs
Finding that balance
Your balance
Is hard
I lose my place
It's always the same
In rage
I smash everything I am
Into pieces
Then I curl up in despair
Slowly
Lovingly
You pick up the pieces
And mend them perfectly
Gently
You take my hand
And we start again

*   *   *

Something About Power ... (1994)

Something about power and the mind
I misunderstand God's creative gift
Nothing has power over me
Unless I decide that it does
I make this decision
I give it power
Without recognizing my error
I create the illusion
Of an external power
And an internal helplessness
This decision can be unmade
If I withdraw the power
I have withdrawn the cause
And the effect disappears
The control over me is gone
Truly
I am free

As I Understand ... (1994)

As I understand this truth
It changes focus
The same truth
A different error
If it is true for power
Is it true for separation
Some place in our consciousness
Did we create an illusion of separation
A mind decision
A mind illusion
Which never really existed
Nothing has ever separated us
We are as we were created
We are one with You
We never left
Truly understood
That means
Our minds are one
Our will is one
Our power is one
Is that our reality
Is that what is
For every living person
I can't begin to comprehend

The Experience ... (1994)

The experience feels the same
To say
Get behind me Satan
Or to tell myself
My illusory self
To get out of the way
And
The result is the same
Are they the same
Satan
Evil
Illusion
Ego

Jesus (1995)

Jesus
Do I understand correctly
Were You the first human
Born without the illusion of separation
You knew Your Source
And Your strength
Being fully aware
Fully conscious
You understood Your divinity
And Your humanity
Dare I ask
How much are we like You
Did You come to show us our abilities
By demonstrating Yours
Because they are the same

It's Hard To See (1995)

It's hard to see
In the darkness of this place
The deep gaping wound
The slashes
It is hell
Where nothing ever heals
Did I create this place
At some time
Did I give life to all of this
Or was it done to me
Are these unforgiven wounds
Or wounds of guilt
You say
Shine My light
And watch the shadows disappear
In truth
This place never was
And never will be
Light and darkness cannot coexist

* * *

This experience occurred during the Consecration at Mass
when the priest held up the bread and said, "This is My Body."
I remember thinking, "I wonder why Jesus did that. What a
strange thing to say. I wonder what He was thinking at that
moment that made Him pick up a piece of bread and say to His
friends, 'This is My Body." My thought ended there and I tried
to move on but the thought was held in place. I remember feeling
as if my thoughts had been given a slight shake. I was aware
enough of it that I stopped and paid attention. Actually, I
remember thinking, "What? What did I miss?" That might
sound disrespectful but it wasn't.

The mood or sense that I have at the time of an experience
is not always the same as what I feel when I am writing about it.
For instance, I recall clearly how serious a moment it was when
I pondered this question later - about Jesus - about His connection
to creation - and ours.

Why ... (1995)

Why did You say that
Why did You hold up bread
And say
This is My Body
And lift a cup of wine
And say
This is My Blood
What were You thinking
What does that mean
To You
If I understand who You were
And who we are
What does that mean
For us

*   *   *

They Recognized You (1995)

They recognized You
In the breaking of the bread
Only then
So
Your words were real
This is My Body
This is My Blood
They didn't recognize the ritual
They recognized Your presence
What did they recognize
What did they understand
What has changed

Choices (1995)

Choices
We misunderstand choices
The axis is wrong
The points of confusion
In front of us
Are symptoms
Reactions
We are choosing
Between fog and shadows
The real choice is between
External
And internal
Where root causes are known
And understood
Where healing is possible
Where guidance is always given
We need only
Bring the question
To the answer

Listen (1995)

Listen
You will hear the need
I will give you the words
I will direct your actions
Be empty
Be still
Be led
Listen

Was Our Sharing ... (1995)

Was our sharing of the cup
A Eucharistic experience
I understand now
What You offered me
Nothing less than everything
All that You are
Truly
I met You
I recognized You
In the sharing of the cup
I know that
I know
This sacred moment never ended
It is

Here (1995)

Here
Now
Pay attention
I am here
Now

In Fleeting Moments (1995)

In fleeting moments
I glimpse Your truth
It almost overwhelms me
If You created me
I come from You
What I know of You
Must also be true of me
It cannot be otherwise
Why do I run from this
Why is it hard to live
Forgiven
Loved
Safe
Perfect
Free
Who we really are
All else is illusion

I Don't Understand (1995)

I don't understand
Yet
How everything that happens
Is illusory
Pain
Illness
Death
I do believe that
If it cannot affect God
Somehow
It cannot affect me
My true self
But
I can't make that work

Some Part Of Me (1995)

Some part of me understands
Somewhere I am
Still
Certain
Waiting
Like the cook with his cleaver
I follow the Spirit
Along the natural line
Through the hidden spaces
The secret openings
I know nothing of

*   *   *

What Did You Want … (1995)

What did You want me to do
What do You want me to do
Why do I hear my own words
I know he's needy
But someone must give love
To people like that
This memory will not fade
Or be resolved
Only one thing has changed
His face is Yours

I was meant to remember this experience clearly - and I do. It almost plays out in slow motion in my mind.

About ten years ago on a day when my daughter had some after-school activity so that I picked her up around supper time, we were driving down the main street of our city when I spotted a man crawling out from the curb on his hands and knees toward the traffic. I pulled over, told my daughter to stay with the car and walked back to him.

We were in front of a bus stop filled with people. I tried to pick the man up myself but I couldn't. I remember feeling confused, not annoyed, about why people wouldn't help him. Then a woman walked over to his other side. The man was elderly, inebriated, crying and sobbing. He uttered his only words as we began to lift him up. I almost burst into tears myself when he said, "I'm a veteran, you know."

We half-carried and half dragged him to a nearby bench and sat him down. There was another man on the bench who also looked homeless.

I said to the other person, "Do you know this man?"

He said, "Oh sure. Don't worry about him. He's just drunk."

My over-riding feeling was relief at seeing someone who knew him, because that meant I could let myself off the hook. "After all," I thought, "I've done my bit."

Meanwhile, the first man continued to sob.

Then the other woman left and I returned to the car. My daughter said, "Mom, you're a good person." I remember looking at her and thinking so many things at once that I said nothing. If I had, I would have started by saying, "There's such a difference between looking good and being good."

I remember my thoughts as I watched the sobbing man in my rear view mirror. I thought, "What a difference I could make in his life - what a profound difference - not with a job and AA meetings, but if I learned his name and his story and his needs. One caring, respectful person could change the quality of this man's life. I have that power. Maybe I could invite him over for Thanksgiving dinner - and Christmas - but how could we welcome him into our home on the 25th - and not the 26th?"

I thought about my family and my responsibilities. After all, I had left dinner cooking, I had a family to feed. They were all counting on me. I took one last glance in the rear view mirror. The man was still crying hard and he had tipped so far forward that I knew he was about to fall off the bench and start crawling again.

I drove away.

* * *

Sometimes (1995)

Sometimes
This gentle journey
Reminds me
Of Jonathon Livingston Seagull
A tiny seed of an idea
A glimmer of understanding
I try it
It works
It falters
It fails
Not quite right
I'm missing something
Let it be
I try again
I have it
I know I have it
Incredible pieces
Gifts beyond measure
That become part of me
I recognize them as true
Another shift
Something new
The graced struggle
Then the quiet certainty
The deep peace of knowing

Which Of Us ... (1995)

Which of us is moving
Are You breaking through
My consciousness
Am I moving into Oneness
And backing off into illusion
This must be
The function of the Spirit
Somehow
The channel between us
Until that is no longer necessary
In the end
Will the Son and Holy Spirit
Fold back into Oneness
Is the trinity
A synonym for life
The reality of life
The Creator
The created
And the Channel between us
What a loving response
To our veil of illusion
Is that how it was
The instant of the veil
Was the instant of the Spirit
The only thing that changed
Was our ability to see
That nothing had changed
Was that the instant of the Big Bang

How Much Do We Know (1995)

How much do we know
How much can we access
On some level
Do we have knowledge
Of everything that has gone before
Not back to our beginning
But back to *the* beginning
Knowledge imprinted
On an unbroken cell-line
A flowing blood line
On our very souls
Do we have the same soul
Is there only one
I wonder

> I dwell for an instant
> In that space beyond words
> It is a living moment
> Someone else is with me
> I connect
> To where I am
> Is that where I was
> Where I will be

If that is the truth
It never changes
If I can be in that place
However briefly
And still be alive
What does that mean
About heaven
What does that mean
About the possibilities of life

*   *   *

Freedom (1995)

Freedom is not of the body
Locked into a space
Confined to a place
Freedom is of the mind
Which soars without limits
Explores without boundaries
Freedom is
Forever safe
Forever untouchable

This poem "Freedom" and the one that follows "How Can I Lose…" are good examples of how I understood and could use, then forgot, then later remembered some aspect of spiritual development. The result is that some poems may appear to be in the wrong sequence but that is not so. They are in the order in which I lived them.

How Can I Lose … (1995)

How can I lose what I know
So quickly
So completely
I am
Physically
Mentally
Trapped by my circumstances
And my mind
I can't climb out of this bog
I forget how to be free

* * *

The Storm (1995)

For days I caught glimpses
Of You sleeping
Through the storm
And I knew
I knew
You were right
They didn't have to awaken You
If they understood their choices
If they remembered what was real
They would know their safety

Will I remember that
When my dark clouds gather

I closed my eyes
I refused to panic
I'm sitting back here
With Jesus
I'm not moving
I'm safe
We're all safe

Threatening clouds swirled
The boat began to pitch
The panic rose

Then
Slowly
Something settled over me

Something deep
Gentle
Calm
Out of sync with everything
Within me
And around me

Remember
I am here
You are safe
I knew it was true

Then
In one incredible instant
The storm reversed
It veered
In amazement
In gratitude
We said
It's a miracle
It was

It was more
I should understand more

Too many words
Too much clutter
I will return to that place
Again and again
Not because I understand
But because I know

*　　*　　*

I No Longer Wonder (1996)

I no longer wonder
Who is helping whom
Who is healing whom
                    You call me
                    To come
                    Alone
                    To join you
                    Where you are
Somehow
I am there
Exposed
Equal
Vulnerable
                    This moment is so real
                    I can't see the past
                    Or imagine the future
                    They mean nothing
                    Less than nothing
Your whole being talks
My whole being listens
I experience your words
I see through your tears
Is it possible
I almost feel your heartbeat
                    My God
                    How could someone
                    So precious
                    Live with such pain
                    No
                    How could we inflict pain

On someone so precious
No
How could I be so blind
As to miss all of this
                I say to myself
                Do I seriously think
                My reality
                Is more real than this
I can't stay here
I don't know how
But I'll be back
                Can you hold my hand
                From this place

    This poem washed over me at a level so deep that I couldn't stop crying. It was the reliving of an experience I described earlier as the first time I sensed a shift in dimension when I chose to listen to someone in great emotional pain - **"I Had A Moment" (1992).**

I Had A Moment (1992)

I had a moment
One awesome moment
Of total presence
Of perfect focus
A place within
Clearly
Someone else
Within my mind
My soul

Within
Or maybe
At one with
In this graced place
I knew the pain
I understood each word
A holy instant
Somehow
I think
A place of miracles

As I write this I recognize the circling, the confusion of my thoughts as I try to understand and describe this experience which continues to draw me.

What I know is that I was the receiver as much as the giver. In fact, this moment felt like a precious gift to me - truly, "A holy instant".

Did I re-enter his pain?

Was he calling to me in my pain?

Was it "our" pain, the same pain?

Who was inviting me into this moment, leading me, teaching me?

What are the possibilities of entering into the pain of another?

I don't have it - yet.

* * *

... I Can Hear You (1996)

Of course I can hear you
Which also means
Of course
There will be a slight delay
As your words
Are processed through my filters
My verdict will arrive
Momentarily
        The fact that I am healthy
        Free
        Educated
        Safe
        White
        Financially secure
        Socially accepted
        Needed
        And loved
        Is irrelevant

Babbling Betty (1996)

I see myself talking words
Babble
I don't have it
Will I ever find that balance
Between attentive listening
Reflective responses
Spontaneity
And silence
I wonder
Is that Betty I recognize

Silently (1996)

Silently
And alone
I read the words
This is My body
Softly
But aloud
I added
And this is my body
Caught by surprise
Again
I wondered how I could speak
What was not yet a thought
Trusting Your guidance
If it was Your guidance
I tried it out
Repeatedly
Deeply
I responded after Your words
And this is my body
It seemed to flow so naturally
It was my amen statement
Of union
Of oneness
Something slipped into place
Things were in their natural order

Is that what you meant
When you said
Do this in remembrance of Me
Showing us how to pray
How to understand our place in creation

Were You saying
Remember what I did
And do likewise

Freedom … (1996)

Freedom cannot be of the mind
Alone
Inaccessible to some
It must come through the Spirit
Be the Spirit
That part of our mind
That we share with God
Is the mind alone
Closed off from truth
Capable only of illusion
Is it opened by the Spirit
Made accessible to all
Filled with possibilities
Capable of reality
Open to eternity

I Place The Pain (1996)

I place the pain
The illness
Of a loved one
On the paten
And ask for transformation
Of his problems
As the bread and wine
Will be transformed

Today
Those words stick in my mind
What am I really saying
Should I be paying more attention
Do I know more

How are the bread and wine transformed
Does the transformation happen
Within me
When I move
From illusion to reality

When I recognize
God
In the bread
The Creator
Truly present
In His creations
I see
What already is
What always is

So what does that mean
For my loved one
Does the transformation of his illness
Happen within me
When I can look at him
And recognize that he is healed
Already
Because his reality is perfection

Does that put the mind of God
In control
Render the body powerless
By being meaningless

Nothing real can be threatened
Nothing unreal exists
Therein lies the peace of God

The peace of God
The state of perfect healing

Please (1996)

Please
Forgive me

I cannot bear
To accept the memories
My assaults on your gentleness

My heart aches
To start again
To hold you tenderly in its care

If I Could Be ... (1996)

If I could be in my world
An open window
Heaven would become visible
Present
Through me
Making healing possible
And natural
My voice
My hands
And my body
Framing the window
Until they disappear
Is that how God must become visible
The way He is seen
Only through us
Once we have removed the obstacles
Which block Him from view

... Butterfly (1996)

A delicate butterfly
In a summer meadow
So right for each other
Not yet
Not quite
The butterfly dips
Hovers
Almost touching the wild flowers
Again and again

A fertilized egg
Brimming with life
Floating in the womb
Conditions are perfect
All that remains
Is the connection

I sense the invitation
Yet I continue to hover
To float
Through the days of my life

One Time (1997)

One time
Mary
I thought about you
Mother to mother
And I cried for your pain
How did you stand
To watch your son
Being put to death
My mind cannot comprehend
That depth of agony
I was overwhelmed by your strength
Your quiet presence
Your acceptance
Because your son accepted
An extraordinary woman
Who knew pain
And understood love

You have always had my respect
And admiration
But not my devotion
I don't know why that is
It just is
But now
After all these years
I wonder
Are you to be my role model
Not Jesus
Or maybe both

When I listened to your story
I heard your fears
And your questions
Again
I marveled at your acceptance
And your faith
Your willingness to be single
Pregnant
Poor
All because you understood
What God asked of you
Incredibly
You didn't just do it
You did it joyfully

I understand
Deeply
You held all these things
In your heart

Is it your example
I must follow
In my own small way
I struggle to understand
To do
Whatever it is
God is asking me to do

Woman to woman
Friend to friend
Mother
Please walk with me
Show me the way

... I Still Wince (1997)

Why do I still wince
At the thought
Of disappearing into the light
In the light
You called me by name
What could be more individual
More personal
Separate
Unique
I experienced
New levels of consciousness
My own thoughts
Feelings
Who I was
Complete
Whole
Myself
How could that not be enough
Something holds me back

A thousand times worse than Thomas

A Darkness … (1997)

A darkness envelopes my mind
The present
Confronts me with the whole
When I can barely survive
One piece
One day at a time
I cannot look into that agonizing blackness
I cannot escape its shadow
It turns color to gray
It deadens my vision
My voice
I'll leave this space
The only way I can
In a ball
Under the covers
Shut down my mind
Wake up in another time

… A Part Of Something (1997)

To be a part of something
Is not to disappear

*   *   *

Something Is Different (1997)

Something is different
For the first time in my life
I feel the early
Tentative
Steps
Trusting myself
Alone
Putting down roots
In who I am
It's always been so easy
To knock me loose
I float after something
Else
Someone
Else
How gently You show me
What I feel
But have yet to understand
Always
You are right
I hover
And float
The connection to be made
Is not to You
But to myself
How can You know all of that
Before I do
Where are You

An image prompted this poem. It was an outline of legs and feet from the back. Inside the margins a cloud-like material almost filled the space, then floated up and down.

As I wrote this poem later, I was surprised by the realization that this image seemed to be the third in a series which included the butterfly and the fertilized egg.

Again I was astonished by the sheer brilliance of these images as gentle, patient teaching tools for me.

Over the years I have used, or maybe abused, words like "mind", "spirit", "psyche" and "God" so much that it's hard to convey what my thoughts and feelings were when these same words took on a new meaning - when they became real at a level so deep it was haunting. This seemed to happen as an extension of that experience. How could it be? These character traits of mine, these unique, personal components of my psyche were being brought to my attention by someone who understood me more than I understood myself. What does that *really* mean? What am I saying? I found myself at the edge of the unknown - again - grasping for the next line or the next question, without success.

What I had understood from reading *A Course in Miracles* was that we underestimate the power of the mind. It seeks to exercise control over us but that power is an illusion. That negative force which teaches and reinforces weakness and limitations could not be the same force leading me to this freedom and understanding.

I feel sure these images were from God - from His Spirit within me. But what does *that* mean? Is it a "someone else" or a "something else" within me? Or is it not a case of "other" at all? Am I the same, one and the same, as this Source of Wisdom which is guiding me and teaching me?

The solution to this deep and awesome mystery eludes me yet, I feel no peace in accepting that fact. My sense is more one of failing to make a connection which is waiting to be made.

*   *   *

2000 Years... (1997)

2000 years later
We struggle to grasp
To accept
Equality
To change all the rules
Totally
This time
It won't go away
Its haunting presence
Resurfaces
Again and again
Equal means equal
Have You waited all this time
For us to understand
Your basic premise
Before we can move on

*   *   *

One morning when I was at Mass these words entered my thoughts - "a celebration of creation." After Mass I tried to write a poem to reflect those words but nothing happened. I seemed to be repeating old ideas so I put the words away. I do that often if I'm stuck on some thought or idea. Eventually, the thought will make sense to me. Over the next few weeks, or maybe longer, I reread the words as I came across them but they still meant nothing so I'd put them away again. Then one day at Mass I read or heard the words "a celebration of the Sacrifice of the Mass." I felt instantly that I had found the connection. I asked myself, "Could it be that the Mass is not a celebration of sacrifice but rather a celebration of creation?" As I went over what I had come to understand it seemed to be a perfect and gentle correction of an error in my thinking.

A Celebration … (1997)

A celebration of creation
Not sacrifice
The same celebrant
The same gifts
The same Offering
Consecration
Eucharist
The same
Yet different
Totally
A profound transformation

* * *

We Are Unique (1997)

We are unique
Perfect
Creations
Extensions
Of God
In
Constant
Loving
Total
Contact
God's gifts
Are ours
To use
To give
Miracles
Are not miracles
They are
Our natural state
I know this
But I don't know how
To know this
And be me

... A Perfect Match (1997)

You have created a perfect match
Who and how I am suits me
This is where I fit
This is the only place I fit
Still I drift away
A chameleon
I please
I appease
I impress
I survive
All my life
I have abandoned my space
At the first sign of trouble

Are You Found ... (1997)

Are You found in the possibilities
Not the events
As these unfold
You are with us
Constant
In strength and power
Reminding us
That we are
Also

These are the words of my faith. (1997)

"BE STILL AND KNOW THAT I AM GOD"

LISTEN

NOW

KNOW

ALREADY

EQUAL

ONE

LOVE

Jesus (1998)

Jesus
There You are
Between heaven and earth
Knowing and understanding God
Knowing and understanding us
Alone
And complete
In that perfect knowledge
How can it be
That You didn't end
You remain above me
In front of me
Beside me
Within me
Always extending
An invitation into reality
So much like the Spirit
I wonder
Is that who You are
The Spirit made visible
What about us
Is that who we are

... So Right (1998)

This feels so right
It seems to flow
Naturally
Am I in trinity
With You
With my Creator
If so
That elevates my life
To a sacred union
It changes who I am
How I see myself
Is that our reality
The Father
Son
And Holy Spirit
The Creator
His creations
And the Spirit which joins us
Somehow
The same words
With a different meaning

... The Expanding Universe (1998)

If the expanding universe
Can be reversed to a point
Can we say the same
About our expanding consciousness

... Our Possibility (1998)

Is that our possibility
To bring about heaven
As we know Your presence
Your love
Your forgiveness
The changes in us
Change what can be seen
And known
Through us
Our human presence
Becomes an opening
Your love flows through us
To another
When the world is full
Of these free-flowing spaces
Will we recognize where we are
Where we have always been

Questions (1998)

Are we the only species
Who need love
Without it
We fail to thrive
            Can we know
            Love and forgiveness
            Only through another
Were we created
To be the presence of love
In creation

                    *   *   *

... One Act of Creation (1998)

Was there only one act of creation
Only one instant
From which everything flows
Could that be the point
Are we the mind
The consciousness
Of the universe
Now able to reflect on itself
Is that who we are
And why we are
Is that where we are going
Toward full understanding
Complete consciousness

There was often a long time lapse, sometimes years, between reading and hearing an idea which I recognized as true or possible and having it become a part of me, become something I knew or understood. That was the case with the possibility that we are the consciousness of the universe.

In "The Global Brain" Peter Russell (18) defines the "GAIA Hypothesis" as the theory "that the earth is one huge self-regulating system." He asks, "Could planet earth be a single living organism?" He goes on to state, "We are the universe's way of beginning to explore itself... the stars' way of exploring the stars..."

All very intriguing and thought-provoking but on the day I wrote this poem I was not, consciously, thinking about anything other than the words of the poem.

* * *

Something Is Changing (1998)

Something is changing
Again
When I am still
And open
My thoughts flow
To You
In an outward motion
But it doesn't work
Somehow
I sense
My words return to me
Or through me
I don't understand this shift
How can I pray to You
Through myself
What does that mean

Jesus Died (1998)

Jesus died
So that sins may be forgiven
Could it be
Jesus lived
So that we may know our forgiveness

We Are One ... (1998)

We are one in spirit
You are with me in spirit
What I do not know is
How safe is my life
You don't ask for sacrifice
Yet You show
My path
Becoming a living cross
My head
Surrounded by thorns
But untouched
What does that mean
For me

Jesus (1998)

Jesus
Do you see illusion
But know truth
Does God see only truth
Do we see only illusion

Quietly (1998)

Quietly
I speak my truth
Lord
You made me worthy to receive You
You said the word
And I am healed

... Trying To Divide (1998)

Am I trying to divide
The indivisible
Do we have one soul
Which is God
Which is us

Life Forms (1998)

Life forms
Unfolds
Disappears
Always repeating
Always expanding
The universal image
Of the human experience

How (1999)

How
Why
Would the Source of love and truth
Create
Sick
Weak
Powerless
Confused people
God created perfectly
Why can't I live what I know
I have choices
My mind judges
Decides
And so it is
My mind dictates
My body follows
When do I choose
Where do I choose
How do I choose

... One Sacred Moment (1999)

For one sacred moment
I remember what IS
And I understand praise

... The Same Cup (1999)

We drink from the same cup
Truly
You are here
What happens to me
Happens to You
You alone
Fully understand
You wait for my invitation
To enter into the moment
And transform it

This truth
Is the rock
The constant
The only constant
Of life

What Am I Missing (1999)

What am I missing
I do not stand
    In the world
    Facing God
    Remembering Him
I stand
    With God
    Knowing Him
    Facing the world
A truth
Beyond my grasp
God is not "other"
The world is not "other"

... This Space (1999)

What is this space
Dark
But not empty
Known physically
Mentally
A space of deep connection
To an unknown now
Where I am present
Able to draw on its depth
Breathe in
A reality
Which renders all else
Irrelevant
Why dark
Is this infinity

Twice I Glimpsed ... (1999)

Twice I glimpsed the pain of another
Through You
Are You always
There

These moments of awareness were painful
Heartbreaking
Both
Are You in constant pain

Do You take on this pain
For us
Inviting
Awaiting
Our awareness

How can You know
Joy and pain
Peace and anguish
At the same time

Something (1999)

Something
Or nothing
Strange mistakes
Unexpected mix-ups
In breathing
Faltering rhythm
Panic

Deep
Slow
Breathing
Peace
In body
Peace
In mind

How Startling (1999)

How startling
How astonishing
10% of me
Known
90%
Unknown
10% of the universe
Known
90%
Unknown
Called dark matter
Is that a coincidence

This Day ... (2000)

This day hasn't happened
The possibilities are staggering

... The Illusion (2000)

Are we the illusion
The barrier
Between our internal
And our external
Universe

But (2000)

But
Do I truly believe
God is present
In everything
In the wheat
In the grapes
In him
In her
In me

*   *   *

This brief image was an event in the distance - something big or bright or loud and a fine, swirling spiral. I'm not sure how to describe the event because, somehow, it was already over in the same instant that I understood it to be happening.

The best comparison I can think of is to visualize the top of an old wooden box slamming, dust swirling. Although the effect lingered, the event really started and ended in that one instant.

That was how I understood this image at the time it happened - and ever since.

... An Instant (2000)

Was it not an instant
From which all life flowed
But
Simply
An instant

Are we still spiralling outward
From that instant
Maybe
In that instant

Is time the illusion

*   *   *

It Circles (2000)

It circles
Nags
Repeats in my mind
Slammed shut
Too similar
The box lid slams
The casket lid slams
What ended
What started

My Body (2001)

My body stumbles
Struggles
I catch myself
About to publicly ridicule
Privately demean
This gift
That is my home
That needs my love
When did I abandon
Even this space

No One (2001)

No one has
An unknown pain

A Moment (2001)

A moment
Of expanded consciousness
The words of my friend
Becoming visible
People walking
They weren't there
Were they

A moment
Of expanded consciousness
A fully alive moment
"Real" life
People walking
They were there
Weren't they

A Strange Awareness (2001)

A strange awareness
Stirring memories
From my youth
Thrilling
Fascinating
Glowing from within
It is possible
Could I be falling in love
All over again

The Instant (2001)

The instant
"The universe bursts into existence" (16)
The instant
Of creation
"Gives birth to space, time
And all the matter and energy
The universe will ever hold" (16)
Could it be
Creation
Complete in that instant
Like the rose in the seed
Are we simply
Unfolding
Spiralling outward
From that instant
Maybe
In that instant

How Can It Be (2001)

How can it be
The most fragile of God's creations
Struggle alone
More precious
More delicate
Than a robin's egg
Who would crush a robin's egg

In Mindful Moments (2001)

In mindful moments
As never before
I am aware
Of our existence
In this living moment
Of You
Of me
Of the possibility of possibilities
Yet
In this free-flowing connection
I falter
I don't see
What You see
The moment passes
Unrealized

Is Now (2002)

Is now
The instant of creation
This timeless space
That always is
How can it be
How can it be otherwise

These are the words of my faith. (1997)

"BE STILL AND KNOW THAT I AM GOD"

LISTEN

NOW

KNOW

ALREADY

EQUAL

ONE

LOVE

While knowing that I am truly and utterly special and unique, I understand absolutely that I am neither special nor unique.

I cannot explain this great mystery but it has been a constant thread running through my experiences.

I hope I have succeeded in imparting my understanding of this miraculous paradox.

Good luck and God bless!

Gail

But (2000)

But
Do I truly believe
God is present
In everything
In the wheat
In the grapes
In him
In her
In me

INDEX OF POEMS

Bibliography

1.   McGuire, J. Leonard - 1927. *Oat-Cakes and Sulphur.* Recorder Printing Co. Ltd., Brockville. 81pp.

2.   Vanier, Jean. 1975. *Be Not Afraid.* Griffin House, Toronto. 145 pp.

3.   Mojtabai, A. G. 1986. *Blessèd Assurance - At Home with the Bomb in Amarillo, Texas.* Houghton Mifflin Company, Boston.

4.   Guided Study Programs in the Catholic Faith. 1978. Journey. The Divine Word International Centre of Religious Education.

5.   Strauss, Stephen. 1988. Biblical exodus a myth, archeologist suggests. Globe and Mail, February 18, 1988.

6.   Bringhurst, Robert. 1988. Myths Create A World of Meaning. Globe and Mail, May 7, 1988.

7.   Compact-N: agreement, covenant. The Merriam Webster Dictionary. 1994. Merriam-Webster, Inc. Springfield, Massachusetts. 891pp.

8.   Greenspan, Louis. 1988. A Judaism that Cuts Across All of the Denominations - Review of "What is Judaism? An Interpretation for the Present Age" by Emil Fackenheim. Globe and Mail, May 14, 1988.

9.   Akenson, Donald H. 1988. The Bible and Ideas of Holy Nationalism - Review of "God Land - Reflection on Religion and Nationalism" by Conor Cruise O'Brien. Globe and Mail, May 14, 1988.

10.   Bergan, Jacqueline Syrup and Schwan, S. Marie. 1985. *Love - A Guide for Prayer*. Saint Mary's Press, Winona, Minnesota. 113pp.

11.   Mandino, Og. 1975. *The Greatest Miracle in the World*. Bantam Books, New York. 108pp.

12.   1976. *A Course in Miracles*. Foundation for Inner Peace, Tiburon, California. Canadian Foundation for Awareness of Miracles (613) 721-0353.

13.   Merton, Thomas. 1965. *The Way of Chuang Tzu*. Shambala, Boston & London. 240pp.

14.   Dostoevsky, Fyodor. 1880. The Grand Inquisitor. From *The Brothers Karamazov*. Penguin Books, New York. 55 pp.

15.   Dilworth, Thomas. 1990. Book Offers Exercises for Christian Living - Review of *A Course in Miracles*. Catholic New Times, Vol. 14, #17, September 23, 1990.

16.   Powell, John. *My Vision and My Values*. Cassette Series.

17.   Lemonick, Michael D. 2001. THE END. TIME magazine. June 25, 2001.

18.   Russell, Peter. 1985. The Global Brain. Video. Hartley Film Foundation Inc., Connecticut. 35 minutes.

19.   Hawking, Stephen W. 1988. *A Brief History of Time - From the Big Bang to Black Holes*. Bantam Books, Toronto. 198 pp.

20.   Nilsson, Lennart. 1990. The First Days of Creation. Life Magazine, August 1990.

ABOUT THE AUTHOR

Gail Higgins: Nurse, mother, poet, peace activist

Gail Higgins was born in Toronto in 1941 and moved to Windsor, Ontario when her father retired from the R.C.M.P. After graduating as a nurse, she moved to Montreal to pursue her interest in Psychiatric Nursing. There she met and married her husband Len, a surgeon, now retired. They have lived in Saint John, New Brunswick for 31 years, raising five children. Two of their sons died in infancy.

Her greatest pleasures are time spent with family and friends, walks in nature in all seasons and quiet reflections on the deck of her summer cottage.